WORD WIZARD

CLASS

Gill SKILLS

Literacy Skills and Activities

Jane O'Loughlin

g GILL EDUCATION

Contents

			Page
How to Use this Book			iv–v
Instructions for Phonics Games			vi

Unit / Genre	Skill	Topic	
UNIT 1: Artwork	Phonics Game	ch, sh, th and wh; ll, ff, ss and zz	1
	Reading, Comprehension, Oral Language	'The Village School' by Jan Steen	2–3
	Phonics	ch, sh, th and wh; ll, ff, ss and zz	4
	Grammar	Capital Letters and Full Stops	5
	Writing Genre	Fact File	6
UNIT 2: Report 1	Phonics Game	sp, st, lt, mp, nd, ck, ng and nk	7
	Reading, Comprehension, Oral Language	The Hedgehog	8–9
	Phonics	sp, st, lt, mp, nd, ck, ng and nk	10
	Grammar	Capital Letters	11
	Writing Genre	Parts of a Report (The Hedgehog)	12
UNIT 3: Report 2	Phonics Game	Magic e with a; Magic e with i	13
	Reading, Comprehension, Oral Language	The Spider	14–15
	Phonics	Magic e with a; Magic e with i	16
	Grammar	Alphabetical Order 1	17
	Writing Genre	Modelled and Shared Writing (The Frog)	18
UNIT 4: Report 3	Phonics Game	Magic e with o; Magic e with u	19
	Reading, Comprehension, Oral Language	Our Skeleton	20–21
	Phonics	Magic e with o; Magic e with u	22
	Grammar	Verbs	23
	Writing Genre	Independent Writing (The Red Squirrel)	24
UNIT 5: Recount 1	Phonics Game	Magic e with blends; /ee/ sound family – ee	25
	Reading, Comprehension, Oral Language	The Day I Bit the Dentist	26–27
	Phonics	Magic e with blends; /ee/ sound family – ee	28
	Grammar	Past Tense Verbs – 'ed'	29
	Writing Genre	Parts of a Recount (and Shared and Modelled Writing)	30
UNIT 6: Recount 2	Phonics Game	/ie/ sound family – ie; /ue/ sound family – ue	31
	Reading, Comprehension, Oral Language	Survey of Favourite Books	32–33
	Phonics	/ie/ sound family – ie; /ue/ sound family – ue	34
	Grammar	Past Tense Irregular Verbs	35
	Writing Genre	Independent Writing (Weekend News)	36
UNIT 7: Recount 3	Phonics Game	/ai/ sound family – ai; /oa/ sound family – oa	37
	Reading, Comprehension, Oral Language	A Letter to Santa	38–39
	Phonics	/ai/ sound family – ai; /oa/ sound family – oa	40
	Grammar	Nouns	41
	Writing Genre	Independent Writing (My Birthday)	42
UNIT 8: Revision and Assessment	Revision	Grammar and Phonics	43–44
	Assessment	Phonics	45
	Reading	The Robin	46
	Assessment	Comprehension and Vocabulary	47
	Assessment	Grammar	48
UNIT 9: Poetry	Phonics Game	/ee/ sound family – ea, y	49
	Reading, Comprehension, Oral Language	'My Puppy' by Aileen Fisher	50–51
	Phonics	/ee/ sound family – ea, y	52
	Grammar	Adjectives 1	53
	Writing Genre	Pyramid Poem	54

Unit / Genre	Skill	Topic	Page
UNIT 10: Narrative 1	Phonics Game	/ou/ sound family – ou; /ur/ sound family – ur	55
	Reading, Comprehension, Oral Language	The Little Red Hen	56–57
	Phonics	/ou/ sound family – ou; /ur/ sound family – ur	58
	Grammar	Past Tense Verbs saw/seen, did/done	59
	Writing Genre	Parts of a Narrative (The Little Red Hen)	60
UNIT 11: Narrative 2	Phonics Game	/ie/ sound family – y (fly), igh	61
	Reading, Comprehension, Oral Language	Under the Bed	62–63
	Phonics	/ie/ sound family – y (fly), igh	64
	Grammar	Alphabetical Order 2	65
	Writing Genre	Modelled and Shared Writing (The Three Billy Goats Gruff)	66
UNIT 12: Narrative 3	Phonics Game	/ue/ sound family – ew; /oi/ sound family – oi	67
	Reading, Comprehension, Oral Language	Snip Snip!	68–69
	Phonics	/ue/ sound family – ew; /oi/ sound family – oi	70
	Grammar	Adjectives 2	71
	Writing Genre	Independent Writing (Jack and the Beanstalk)	72
UNIT 13: Procedure 1	Phonics Game	/ou/ sound family – ow; /ai/ sound family – ay	73
	Reading, Comprehension, Oral Language	How to Make a Flower Mobile	74–75
	Phonics	/ou/ sound family – ow; /ai/ sound family – ay	76
	Grammar	'Bossy' (Command) Verbs	77
	Writing Genre	Parts of a Procedure (How to Make a Flower Mobile)	78
UNIT 14: Procedure 2	Phonics Game	/au/ sound family – aw; /ur/ sound family – ir	79
	Reading, Comprehension, Oral Language	How to Plant Seeds	80–81
	Phonics	/au/ sound family – aw; /ur/ sound family – ir	82
	Grammar	a or an?	83
	Writing Genre	Modelled and Shared Writing (How to Make an Irish Flag)	84
UNIT 15: Procedure 3	Phonics Game	/oi/ sound family – oy; /au/ sound family – au	85
	Reading, Comprehension, Oral Language	'The Gosling Song' by Tony Mitton	86–87
	Phonics	/oi/ sound family – oy; /au/ sound family – au	88
	Grammar	Plural – 'es'	89
	Writing Genre	Independent Writing (How to Make a Spring Chick)	90
UNIT 16: To Socialise 1	Vocabulary	Revision of Homophones	91
	Reading, Comprehension, Oral Language	Butterfly Hill Farm (Advertisement)	92–93
	Phonics	/au/ sound family – al; /ur/ sound family – er	94
	Grammar	Future Tense Verbs 1	95
	Writing	Parts of an Invitation (Invitation to a School Tour)	96
UNIT 17: To Socialise 2	Vocabulary	Revision of Homophones	97
	Reading, Comprehension, Oral Language	Holiday Checklist	98–99
	Phonics	/or/ sound family – or	100
	Grammar	Future Tense Verbs 2	101
	Writing	Independent Writing (Invitation to a Sports Day)	102
UNIT 18: Revision and Assessment	Revision	Grammar and Phonics	103–104
	Assessment	Phonics	105
	Reading	Flat Stanley	106
	Assessment	Comprehension and Vocabulary	107
	Assessment	Grammar	108
Dictation			109–110

How to Use this Book

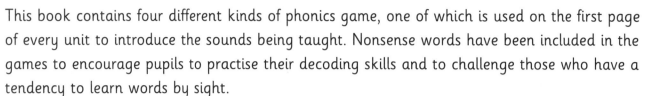

Phonics games

This book contains four different kinds of phonics game, one of which is used on the first page of every unit to introduce the sounds being taught. Nonsense words have been included in the games to encourage pupils to practise their decoding skills and to challenge those who have a tendency to learn words by sight.

A monkey or a raccoon character appears at the bottom of the page, offering tips on how to replay the game at home to further consolidate learning.

Detailed instructions for playing the phonics games can be found on page vi.

Phonics linked with comprehension

Vocabulary containing the sounds taught within the unit has been incorporated into the comprehension reading passages wherever possible. This helps to bridge the gap between phonics and real reading practice, rather than teaching both in isolation. An owl character appears before each reading passage, asking pupils to look out for certain sounds in the text.

Vocabulary development

A meerkat character appears before each reading passage, asking pupils to explain the bold words in the text to their partner before reading. This is designed to facilitate the teaching of tricky vocabulary prior to reading the text.

Higher order comprehension questions

At this level, pupils are being introduced to answering written, lower order thinking questions. In order to ensure that higher order thinking skills are not overlooked, a list of questions is provided online for each reading passage, allowing teachers to develop these skills orally.

Genre writing

The *Word Wizard* series takes a unique approach to genre writing. The reading passage serves as a template for the genre. The teacher can refer to this while outlining the parts (structure) of the genre, by asking pupils to highlight or use yellow stickies to identify various elements. Discrete oral language activities act as building blocks for genre writing, and grammar activities are linked to the genre wherever appropriate.

At this level, genre writing follows a six-week approach, with a fortnight spent on each unit. Generally, three units are dedicated to each genre as follows: the first explores the parts of the genre, the second presents both modelled and shared writing experiences and the third gives pupils an opportunity to write independently. (Please note that recount writing differs somewhat.)

Detailed teaching notes are available online, outlining the steps for progressing through each of the stages. YouTube links have been included to act as a stimulus for writing wherever appropriate.

Dictation

Two dictation sentences are provided for each unit, incorporating the phonics and grammar taught. Suggestions are provided for extension activities or further revision of grammar. Differentiation is also catered for.

Assessment

A self-assessment feature appears below each dictation activity.

Two units dedicated to revision and assessment are provided at the end of the second and third terms. Each includes a special four-day section designed to prompt meaningful revision of phonics and grammar before assessment begins.

Editable writing frames and self-assessment checklists

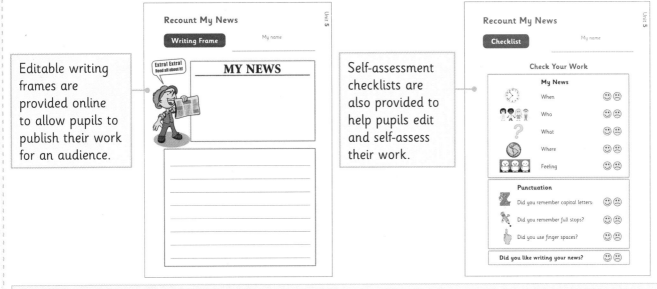

Editable writing frames are provided online to allow pupils to publish their work for an audience.

Self-assessment checklists are also provided to help pupils edit and self-assess their work.

Key to online resource symbols

	Higher order comprehension questions	Indicates that a list of higher order thinking questions is available online.
	Oral language	Indicates that a detailed oral language activity is available online.
	Discussion genre text	Indicates that an excerpt from another text, highlighting features of a particular genre, and accompanying teacher's notes are available online.
	Modelled or shared writing experience	Indicates that a modelled writing activity with accompanying teacher's notes is available online or that the activity book itself presents an opportunity for a shared writing activity. (Please note that most shared writing activities do not come with teacher's notes. These follow on from modelled writing activities, in which the teacher acts as scribe while the class contributes ideas.)
	Printable	Both a writing template and a self-assessment checklist for each genre are available online.

Instructions for Phonics Games

Take me to the...

What you will need:

- two players
- a die

How to play

1. Practise reading all of the words before you begin.
2. Place your counters on start.
3. Roll the die. The player with the highest number goes first.
4. Take turns rolling the die and moving the correct number of places.
5. Sound out each word that you land on.
6. If you read it correctly, you may stay there. If you read it incorrectly, you must go back to where you were.
7. If you land on a star, take another turn.
8. The winner is the first player to reach the finish line.

Snakes and Ladders

What you will need:

- two players
- a die
- two counters

How to play

1. Practise reading all of the words before you begin.
2. Place your counters on start.
3. Roll the die. The player with the highest number goes first.
4. Take turns rolling the die and moving the correct number of places.
5. Sound out each word that you land on.
6. If you land on a ladder, move up.
7. If you land on a snake, move down.
8. The winner is the first player to reach the finish line.

Catch the...

What you will need:

- two players
- a die
- two pencils

How to play

1. Practise reading all of the words before you begin.
2. Place your counters on start.
3. Roll the die. The player with the highest number goes first.
4. Take turns rolling the die and moving the correct number of places.
5. Sound out each word that you land on.
6. If you land on a picture, you must find the word in the middle area of the game and cover it with a counter.
7. The winner is the player who covers the last word with a counter.

A spin and a roll

What you will need:

- two players
- a die
- two pencils

How to play

1. Practise reading all of the words before you begin.
2. Roll the die. The player with the highest number goes first.
3. They must read any word from the column that corresponds to the number on the die. If they read it correctly, they can ring the word.
4. The second player takes their turn.
5. The winner is the first player to ring all of the words in a column.

Teacher's Notes

Section A introduces sounds taught in the unit and recaps on sounds from earlier units. Please note that not all of these sounds are incorporated into the game.

The following suggestions can help to ensure that the words in the game are read correctly:

- Read all of words as a whole-class activity before playing the game.
- Model playing the game in pairs, demonstrating how pupils should read the word that their partner has landed on in order to check that their partner has read it correctly.
- Divide pupils into reading groups. Sit with the weakest group most of the time, but visit another group. The game could be played for a short period on three consecutive days.
- The game could be assigned for homework.

'The Village School'

Phonics Game | ch, sh, th and wh | ll, ff, ss and zz

A Before you begin the game, tick (✓) the sounds that you can read.

ch ✓	ff ✓	cr ✓	ll ✓	sn ✓	th ✓	sh ✓
tr ✓	sm ✓	zz ✓	ss ✓	cl ✓	bl ✓	pl ✓

B Take me to the homework pass!

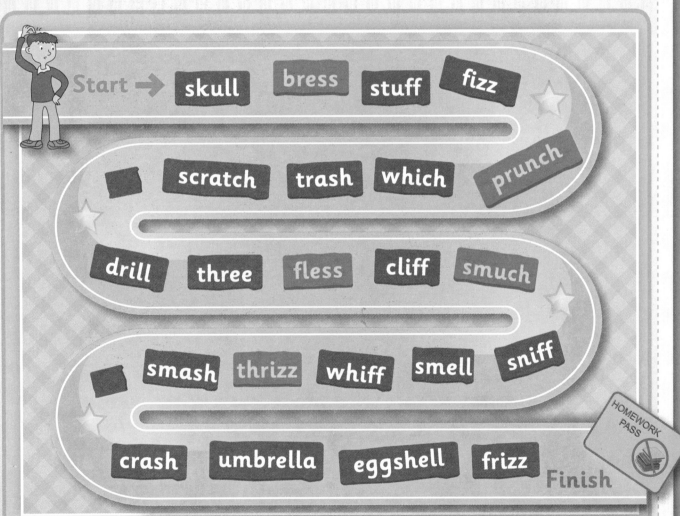

Start → skull bress stuff fizz

scratch trash which prunch

drill three fless cliff smuch

smash thrizz whiff smell sniff

crash umbrella eggshell frizz Finish

HOMEWORK PASS

Try playing this at home again. All you need is a die and a set of counters.

Strand: Reading Element: Understanding LO 4, 5

Looking at Art – 'The Village School'

'*The Village School*' was painted by Jan Steen. He was an artist who lived in Holland a long time ago. This is a painting of a classroom. There are children in the painting. The teacher is looking at the children's work, but he is cross. He is hitting the boy with a wooden spoon. The boy's work is on the floor. Some of the other children are watching. One girl is laughing. Can you find her?

A Write 'yes' or 'no' for each sentence.

1. The teacher has a quill on his desk.
2. The girl is sad.
3. The teacher is mad.
4. The children are at school.
5. The teacher is hitting the boy with a stick.
6. Do you think the children like school?

B Fill in the correct word.

Holland   artist   painted

1. Jan Steen was an _____.
2. He _____ pictures.
3. He lived in _____.

C Vocabulary: Write the correct word.

to

two

1. I had _____ buns.
2. He got _____ sweets.
3. I went _____ the shop.
4. I gave the book _____ him.

Phonics | ch, sh, th and wh | ll, ff, ss and zz

A Look at the picture. Write ✓ or ✗ for each sentence.

1. The children sit on chairs.

2. The teacher sits on a stool.

3. The green frog is in a hutch.

4. The pet fish are in the bath.

5. The shark wants to eat the fish.

6. The brush is in the rubbish bin.

7. There is a skull on the bench.

8. The teacher has a bunch of fresh bananas for lunch.

9. Do you think the teacher will eat the snail for lunch?

Strand: Reading **Element:** Understanding LO 4, 5

Grammar – Capital Letters and Full Stops

We put a capital letter at the start of a sentence.
We put a full stop at the end of a sentence.
Example: **D**ad put the tools in the shed.

A Write the capital letter for each letter below.

a    e   h    n    b

f _____   r    j    q    m

B Read each sentence. Ring what is missing, a capital letter or a full stop.

1. the dog ran away.
2. a cat sat on the big, red mat.
3. I like to swim in the pool
4. mum gave me a book
5. "i do not like sweets," shouted the little boy.
6. she put the doll in the pram

C Dictation: Listen to your teacher and write the sentences.

1. _____

2. _____

How did you do? 🙂 ⚪ 😐 ⚪ 🙁 ⚪

Writing Genre – Fact File

A Fill in your profile below.

My Profile

This is me. Draw a picture of yourself.

What I like best about school

_____

_____

What I like least about school

_____

_____

What I would like to learn about this year

_____

_____

I am _____ years old.

Facts

School: _____

Class: _____

Teacher: _____

People who help us in school

Secretary: _____

Caretaker: _____

Cleaner: _____

My friends

Draw a picture of you and your friends.

Strand: Writing **Elements:** Communicating LO 1, 2; Exploring and Using LO 6, 7

The Hedgehog

2

Phonics Game | **sp, st, lt, mp, nd, ck, ng** and **nk** final consonant blends

A Before you begin the game, tick (✓) the sounds that you can read.

lt		sp		nt		sp		ck		tr	
ng		ch		ss		nk		nd		st	
mp		pl		ff		zz		bl		gr	

B Snakes and Ladders

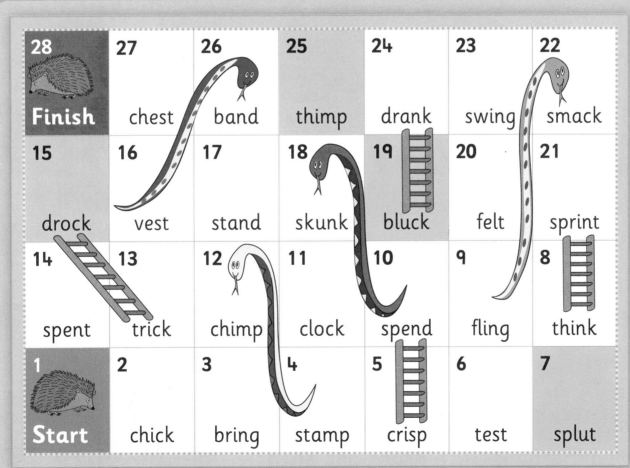

28 Finish	27 chest	26 band	25 thimp	24 drank	23 swing	22 smack
15 drock	16 vest	17 stand	18 skunk	19 bluck	20 felt	21 sprint
14 spent	13 trick	12 chimp	11 clock	10 spend	9 fling	8 think
1 Start	2 chick	3 bring	4 stamp	5 crisp	6 test	7 splut

Try playing this at home again. All you need is a die and a set of counters.

Comprehension

Do you know what the **bold** words below mean? Can you explain them to your partner?

Look out for words with **nd**, **nt**, **st** or **ck** in the report below.

STOP

The Hedgehog

spines

body

snout

feet

The hedgehog is a very small mammal.

The hedgehog has a small, round body.
Its back has **stiff**, sharp **spines**. These are called quills.

You might find hedgehogs in your garden. They like to sleep in nests under thick bushes. They make their nests with leaves, grass and **moss**.

Hedgehogs like to eat snails, slugs, frogs and insects. They sleep all day and hunt when it is dark. They **grunt** and **sniff** when they hunt for food.

They go for a very long sleep in winter. This is called **hibernation**.

Strand: Reading **Elements:** Communicating LO 1; Understanding LO 4, 5, 6

A Answer the questions.

1. Where do hedgehogs make their nests?

Hedgehogs make _____

2. What do they use to make their nests?

They use _____

3. What do they eat?

They eat _____

4. When do they hunt?

They go hunting _____

B Fill in the correct word.

sleep   animal   insects   hunt   grass

1. The hedgehog is a small, round _____ .

2. The hedgehog makes a nest with leaves and _____ .

3. Hedgehogs _____ , or hibernate in winter.

4. When it is dark, they go out and _____ .

5. They eat slugs, snails and _____ .

C Vocabulary: Write the correct word.

1. The dog ran over _____ .

2. They put on _____ coats.

3. Can you put the box over _____ ?

4. That is _____ cat.

5. _____ dog is named Max.

there

their

Phonics sp, st, lt, mp, nd, ck, ng and nk final consonant blends

A Look at each picture. Tick (✓) the correct word.

	block ☐		string ☐		scamp ☐
	blank ☐		stamp ☐		skimp ☐
	black ✓		strong ☐		skunk ☐
	bump ☐		sand ☐		pump ☐
	bring ☐		stand ☐		paint ☐
	brick ☐		send ☐		pond ☐
	cramp ☐		check ☐		bump ☐
	camp ☐		chest ☐		belt ☐
	crisps ☐		chimp ☐		band ☐
	click ☐		nest ☐		sunk ☐
	cluck ☐		mend ☐		sank ☐
	clock ☐		much ☐		sink ☐

B Write the correct word.

1. A frog swims in a _____. **pump / pond / paint**

2. I like to _____ a glass of milk. **drink / dust / dump**

3. A queen bee can _____ you. **struck / sting / string**

4. I _____ my pocket money. **spring / speck / spent**

5. Butter will _____ in the sun. **melt / mend / muck**

Strand: Reading Element: Understanding LO 4, 5

Grammar – Capital Letters

We use capital letters for...

	Examples:
1. names of **people**	Sam, Fred, Dad, Gran
2. names of **places**	Dublin, Belfast, Paris
3. **days** of the week	Sunday, Monday
4. **months** of the year	September, November

DUBLIN   50 km

A Ring the words that need a capital letter.

1. run   mad   (sam)

2. seeds   monday   sad

3. october   big   digger

4. spain   pamela   jeep

August
September
October
Monday
Tuesday
Wednesday
Thursday
Friday
Saturday
Sunday
Beth

B Write the sentences correctly.

1. today is monday

_____

2. we start school in september

_____

3. we went on a trip to dublin zoo

_____

C Dictation: Listen to your teacher and write the sentences.

1. _____

2. _____

How did you do? ☺ ○ ☹ ○ ☹ ○

Writing Genre – Parts of a Report

A Highlight the parts of a report.

Turn back to the report, 'The Hedgehog' on page 8. Use yellow stickies or a highlighter pen to highlight the different parts of the report.

B Fill in the correct words.

| photograph | where they live | what they look like |
| title | diagram with labels | what they eat |

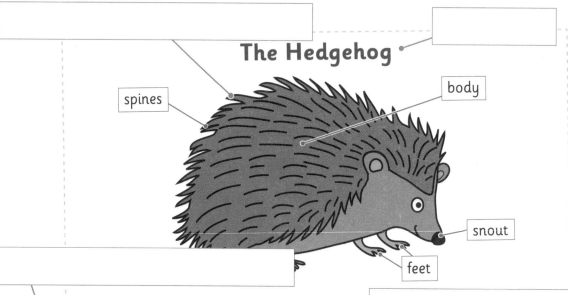

The Hedgehog

spines

body

snout

feet

The hedgehog is a very small mammal.

The hedgehog has a small, round body.
Its back has **stiff**, sharp **spines**. These are called quills.

You might find hedgehogs in your garden. They like to sleep in nests under thick bushes. They make their nests with leaves, grass and **moss**.

Hedgehogs like to eat snails, slugs, frogs and insects. They sleep all day and hunt when it is dark. They **grunt** and **sniff** when they hunt for food.

They go for a very long sleep in winter. This is called **hibernation**.

Strand: Writing Elements: Communicating LO 1; Exploring and Using LO 8

The Spider

Phonics Game | Magic **e** with **a** | Magic **e** with **i**

A Before you begin the game, tick (✓) the sounds that you can read.

i_e		ff		sm		th		ck		zz		a_e	
lt		ll		a_e		mp		i_e		sh		a_e	

B Catch the spiders!

Start →	bive		hame	dake	
afe	kite		five		mide
ine	dive		game		hile
kafe	cake		case		jate
dite					nime
lave		fike	zale	mafe	

Try playing this at home again. All you need is a die and a set of counters.

Strand: Reading Element: Understanding LO 4, 5

Comprehension

STOP

Do you know what the **bold** words below mean? Can you explain them to your partner?

Look out for words that have Magic **e** with **a** or Magic **e** with **i** in the report below.

The Spider

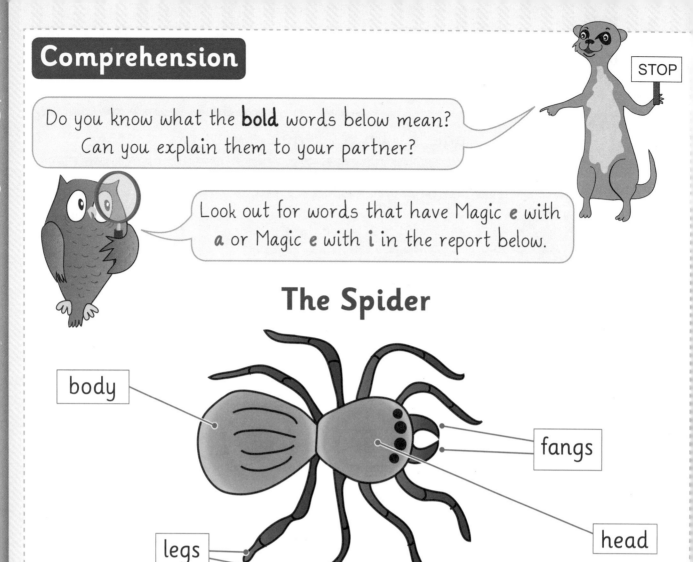

body

fangs

head

legs

A spider is not an insect. An insect has six legs, but a spider has eight legs.

Spiders are different sizes. A spider's legs are very thin. It has **fangs** too.

Spiders live everywhere. They live in trees, under rocks, in caves and even in our houses and gardens.

A spider eats insects. It makes a web to catch them. It spins the web with **silk**. The silk is very strong. It is also very

A spiderweb

fine. The spider can spin the web in a bush or between two plant **stems**. The spider hides in the web and catches insects inside it. It rushes to the insect and bites it with its fangs.

A Answer the questions.

1. How many legs does a spider have?

   <u>A spider</u>

2. Where do spiders live?

   <u>Spiders live</u>

3. What do spiders eat?

   <u>Spiders eat</u>

4. How does a spider bite insects?

   <u>A spider bites insects</u>

5. Do you like spiders? Why/Why not?

   _____

B Write the correct word.

1. A spider is not an _____ . **bee / insect**

2. A spider has _____ legs and fangs. **thin / fat**

3. Spiders catch _____ in their webs. **frogs / insects**

4. Spiders make webs by spinning _____ . **silk / stem**

C Vocabulary: Write the correct word.

to	two	too

1. I have a pet cat _____ .

2. I had _____ bananas for lunch.

3. Can I have some cake _____ ?

4. I gave the bag _____ my dad.

Phonics | Magic **e** with **a** | Magic **e** with **i**

A Look at each picture. Tick (✓) the correct word.

	game gate ✓ gave		safe sale save
	wife wine wire		nine name made
	fake fame five		tape time take
	ride rise rake		cave case cape

B Write the correct word.

1. I like to ride my big, red _____ . **bake / bite / bike**

2. Mum always _____ the sweets. **hides / hikes / hates**

3. Mike _____ Dave a bag of toffees. **gate / game / gave**

4. Gran likes to _____ pancakes. **make / made / maze**

5. I _____ to bring my kite to the park. **late / lane / like**

6. Dad took a big bite out of the _____ . **cake / came / kite**

7. What _____ is your birthday? **dive / date / take**

Strand: Reading Element: Understanding LO 4, 5

Grammar – Alphabetical Order 1

a, b, c, d, e, f, g, h, i, j, k, l, m, n, o, p, q, r, s, t, u, v, w, x, y, z

A Which letter comes next?

1. a, b, c, d, e, f, 　　2. j, k, l, m, n, o,

3. c, d, e, f, g, h, 　　4. p, q, r, s, t, u,

5. s, t, u, v, w, x, 　　6. m, n, o, p, q, r,

B Which letter goes before?

1. ___, b, c 　　2. ___, h, i 　　3. ___, k, l

4. ___, m, n 　　5. ___, s, t 　　6. ___, x, y

7. ___, f, g 　　8. ___, q, r 　　9. ___, t, u

C Ring the word that comes first in alphabetical order.

1. pot 　　spoon 　　(cup)

2. nail 　　tool 　　hammer

3. jeep 　　train 　　van

4. sheep 　　hen 　　fox

5. pram 　　bib 　　cot

6. bee 　　ant 　　snail

7. yellow 　　red 　　blue

D Dictation: Listen to your teacher and write the sentences.

1. _____

2. _____

How did you do?

Strand: Writing Element: Understanding LO 3, 4, 5

Writing Genre – Modelled and Shared Writing

A Complete the fact file.

Read each fact about frogs. Rewrite it in the correct box in the fact sheet.

Facts About Frogs

1. many are green
2. amphibians
3. patterns on skin
4. in ponds and on land
5. short front legs
6. long back legs
7. eat insects, spiders, slugs and snails
8. spend winter at bottom of ponds

Fact Sheet About Frogs

What are they?

What do they look like?

Where do they live?

What do they eat?

B With your class, write a report about frogs.

Strand: Writing Elements: Communicating LO 1; Understanding LO 5; Exploring and Using LO 6, 7

Our Skeleton

Phonics Game | Magic **e** with **o** | Magic **e** with **u**

A Before you begin the game, tick (✓) the sounds that you can read.

u_e	bl	nd	o_e	u_e	a_e	i_e
lt	zz	ch	u_e	sw	ck	o_e

B A spin and a roll

We all say nonsense words!

note	fode	bone	rube	fire	yide
woke	hude	name	jite	rose	fuke
home	dute	wide	foke	cute	doke
rude	pume	hose	vame	cube	lafe
June	sime	rule	mupe	case	zule
gave	bafe	tube	rone	those	nize
kite	cose	joke	bave	doze	hume

Try playing this with two players at home. Simply rub out the words you have ringed in class. This time, Player One can underline words and Player Two can ring them. Whoever fills a column first wins!

Strand: Reading Element: Understanding LO 4, 5

Comprehension

Do you know what the **bold** words below mean? Can you explain them to your partner?

STOP

Look out for words that have Magic **e** with **o** or Magic **e** with **u** in the report below.

Our Skeleton

Our skeleton is made up of lots of bones. You can feel your bones under your skin.

Bones are hard on the outside and soft on the inside. They can be different shapes and sizes. Bones include our **skull**, **spine**, arms, legs, feet and many more.

Most of our body parts are **squishy** and soft. Our skeleton helps to make our body strong, so we do not look like a big blob.

X-ray machines help doctors to see our bones. If you broke your arm, you would put on a **sling**. If you broke your leg, you would use **crutches** or a wheelchair.

Most of our bones are in our hands and feet.

skull

arms

spine

bones

legs

feet

Strand: Reading **Elements:** Communicating LO 1; Understanding LO 4, 5, 6

A Answer the questions.

1. What is our skeleton made of?

Our skeleton is made _____

2. Can you name some of our bones?

_____

3. What machine does a doctor use to see our bones?

A doctor uses _____

4. Where do we find most of our bones?

Most of our bones are _____

B Fill in the correct word.

strong   bones   small   sling

1. Our skeleton is made up of lots of _____ .

2. Some bones are big and some are _____ .

3. Our skeleton helps to make our body _____ .

4. If you broke your arm, you would use a _____ .

C Vocabulary: Write the correct word.

I thought there were three buns left.

were

1. _____ is the shop?

2. I know _____ the park is.

3. The cats _____ in the shed.

4. The children _____ sad.

where

Phonics | Magic **e** with **o** | Magic **e** with **u**

A Tick (✓) the correct word for each sentence.

1. This is a shape.

cube ☐   cute ✓   came ☐   code ☐

2. A king puts this on.

rode ☐   rope ☐   robe ☐   rude ☐

3. A dog eats this.

bake ☐   bone ☐   bike ☐   bite ☐

4. You keep this in a shed or garden.

hope ☐   home ☐   hose ☐   hole ☐

5. You can play games on this.

code ☐   cone ☐   cube ☐   computer ☐

B Write the correct word.

1. Dad _____ the cake that Mum baked.   **cut / cute**

2. I put on my bath _____.   **rob / robe**

3. A baby fox is called a _____.   **cub / cube**

4. I need a _____ of toothpaste.   **tub / tube**

5. I _____ we get no homework.   **hop / hope**

6. I will _____ run in the shop.   **not / note**

7. Yesterday, I _____ my bike to the park.   **rod / rode**

8. Dad had to sweep and _____ the floor.   **mop / mope**

Strand: Reading Element: Understanding LO 4, 5

Grammar – Verbs

Verbs are doing words. They tell us what is happening.

Examples: clap   sing   yell

A Match each picture to the correct verb.

   drink   paint

   jump      sleep

          think   run

B Ring the verb in each sentence.

1. Tom hung up his coat.

2. The kitten fell off the log.

3. I dropped the tray of glasses.

4. I like to ride my bike in the park.

5. Did you take the bag of sweets?

6. I made a chocolate cake last night.

7. I wake up at seven o'clock every morning.

8. Emily kicked her football around the garden

C Dictation: Listen to your teacher and write the sentences.

1. _____

2. _____

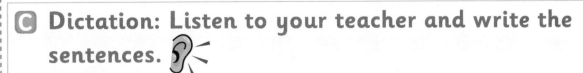

How did you do? ☺ ○   ☹ ○   ☹ ○

Strand: Writing **Element:** Understanding LO 3, 4, 5

Writing Genre – Independent Writing

Ⓐ Complete the fact file.

Read each fact about the red squirrel. Rewrite it in the correct box in the fact sheet.

Facts About the Red Squirrel

1. sharp teeth

2. a small mammal

3. red, bushy tail

4. hibernates in winter

5. eats seeds, nuts and insects

6. lives in a nest called a drey

7. makes nest in a hole in a tree

8. wakes in spring

Fact Sheet About the Red Squirrel

What is it? ❓

What does it look like?

Where does it live? 🏠

What does it eat?

Ⓑ Write a report about the red squirrel by yourself. Include a title and write five sentences.

Ⓒ Look over your report again. Did you remember everything?

Strand: Writing **Elements:** Communicating LO 1; Understanding LO 5; Exploring and Using LO 6, 7

The Day I Bit the Dentist 5

Phonics Game | Magic **e** with blends | /**ee**/ sound family – **ee**

A Before you begin the game, tick (✓) the sounds that you can read.

ee		o_e		a_e		u_e		i_e		ee	
ss		mp		cr		ee		dr		tr	

B Take me to the dentist!

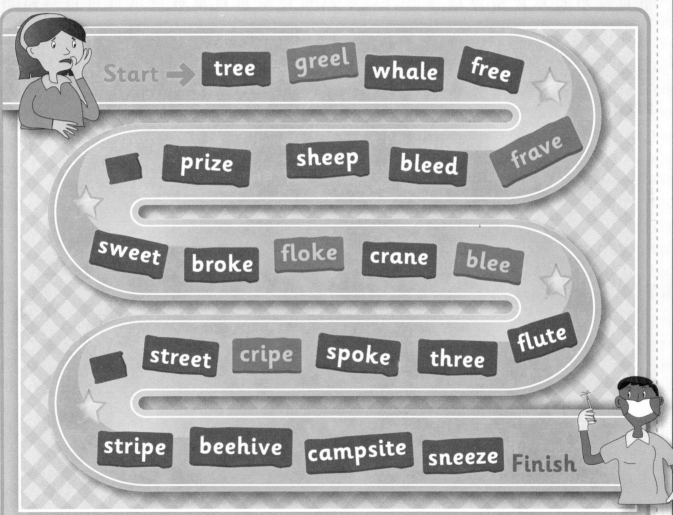

Start → tree greel whale free

prize sheep bleed frave

sweet broke floke crane blee

flute

street cripe spoke three

stripe beehive campsite sneeze Finish

Try playing this at home again. All you need is a die and a set of counters.

Strand: Reading Element: Understanding LO 4, 5

Comprehension

Do you know what the **bold** words below mean? Can you explain them to your partner?

STOP

Look out for words with **ee** in the recount below.

The Day I Bit the Dentist

Okay, okay, I bit the dentist. I didn't mean to.

It all happened last week when I went to the dentist with my mum. I had a bad pain in my tooth. First, I had to sit up on the dentist's chair. Then, the dentist took a look inside my mouth. It was all going okay until he put the **needle** in my **gum**. I didn't **expect** such a **pinch**. Suddenly my cheeks felt all funny. I didn't know what I was doing! My teeth just closed by themselves! The dentist jumped and yelled, "What are you doing?"

Hey, I'm a child. I'm only seven and I had never seen a needle like that before. I didn't know I'd bite him. I didn't know there would be such a **fuss**. Mum was upset and the dentist was very cross. "Oh no," I thought, "get me out of here NOW!"

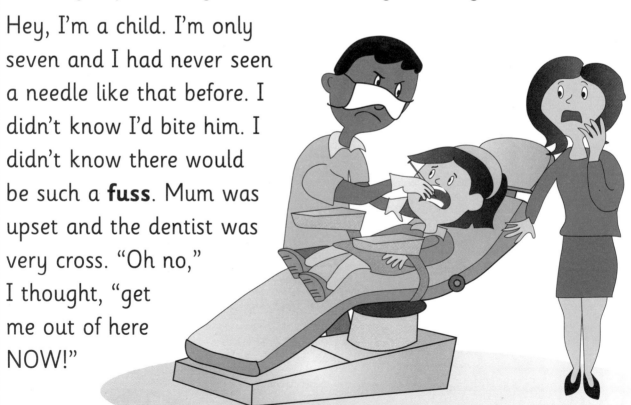

Strand: Reading **Elements:** Communicating LO 1; Understanding LO 4, 5, 6

A Write 'yes' or 'no' for each sentence.

1. The girl bit the dentist.

2. The dentist looked at her neck.

3. Her cheeks felt red.

4. The girl had a pain in her tooth.

B Answer the questions.

1. When did the girl go to the dentist?

_____

2. Who went with her to the dentist?

_____

3. Where did the girl sit?

_____

4. How did she feel when the dentist put the needle in her gum?

_____

5. Do you like going to the dentist? Why/Why not?

_____

C Oral language

Watch your teacher telling his/her news using the planning grid below. In pairs, take turns telling your news.

When	Who	What
Where	**Why**	**Feeling**

Strand: Reading Elements: Understanding LO 5; Exploring and Using LO 8, 9
Strand: Oral Language Elements: Communicating LO 1, 2, 3; Exploring and Using LO 11, 13, 14

27

Phonics | Magic e with blends | /ee/ sound family – ee

A Look at each picture. Tick (✓) the correct word.

	sleep		sweep		cheep
	sheet		sweet		cheek
	sheep ✓		seek		coffee
	sixteen		broke		spade
	fifteen		bride		spoke
	nineteen		blame		spike
	grave		flute		cave
	green		flake		crane
	globe		fluke		crate
	chose		three		stripe
	chase		teeth		steel
	choke		toffee		street
	smoke		beep		screech
	smile		bleep		speech
	sweep		bleed		sneeze

B Read the real and silly words. Tick (✓) the real word in each box.

skate	✓	smute		tree		creef	
blate		slize		streep		wheem	
brame		speed		smeel		freeze	
floke		snuke		sleeve		gride	
close		drove		fleeb		sweex	
frove		crute		bruke		slide	

Strand: Reading **Element:** Understanding LO 4, 5

Grammar – Past Tense Verbs –'ed'

A Do you remember verbs? Ring the verbs in the grid below.

sweets	chair	sit	dentist	close
mouth	bite	eat	drink	lips

The past tense is what happened yesterday.

Sometimes we add 'ed' to the verb.

If a word already ends in 'e' we drop the 'e' and add 'ed'.

Examples: jump – jump**ed**   like – lik**ed**

B Write these verbs in the past tense.

1. cook   **2.** smile   **3.** lock

4. jump   **5.** pick   **6.** shave

C Write these sentences in the past tense by changing the verb in brackets.

1. Gran (park) the jeep in the car park.

_____

2. Seth (bake) some toffee muffins.

_____

3. Mum (look) after the baby.

_____

D Dictation: Listen to your teacher and write the sentences.

1. _____

2. _____

How did you do? ☺ ◯ ☺ ◯ ☹ ◯

Writing Genre – Parts of a Recount

A Plan your news.

Use the news planner to plan your news. Include pictures and words to help you.

News Planner

When	Who	What

Where	Why	Feeling

B As a class, pick one person's news to write together.

Strand: Writing **Elements:** Communicating LO 1, 2; Exploring and Using LO 6, 7, 8

Survey of Favourite Books 6

Phonics Game | /ie/ sound family – **ie** | /ue/ sound family – **ue**

A Before you begin the game, tick (✓) the sounds that you can read.

ue		ee		ie		i_e		ee		u_e
nk		sh		ue		a_e		ck		o_e
ie		lt		ee		ch		ue		ie

B Snakes and Ladders

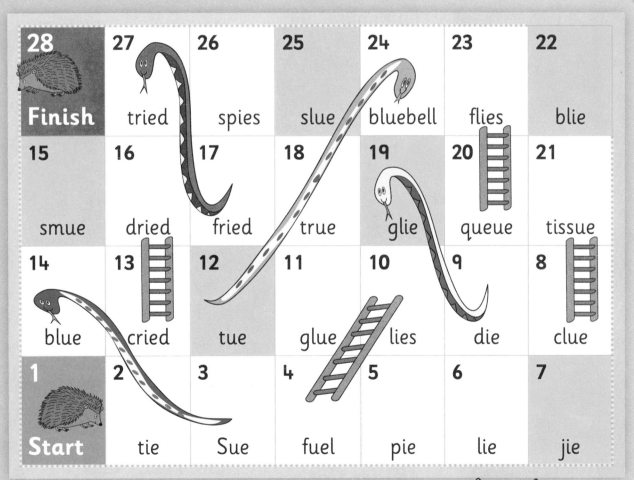

28 Finish	27 tried	26 spies	25 slue	24 bluebell	23 flies	22 blie
15 smue	16 dried	17 fried	18 true	19 glie	20 queue	21 tissue
14 blue	13 cried	12 tue	11 glue	10 lies	9 die	8 clue
1 Start tie	2 Sue	3 fuel	4 pie	5 lie	6	7 jie

Try playing this at home again. All you need is a die and a set of counters.

Comprehension

Survey of Favourite Books

Book	Who liked this book?
'The Cat in the Hat' by Dr Seuss	Bob, Kate, Jane, Dave, Luke, Anna, Sam, Sue
'The Twits' by Roald Dahl	Ken, Jack, Alan, Tom, Bob, Jacob, Abbas, Abdul, Han, Bill
'Fantastic Mr Fox' by Roald Dahl	Jan, Dana, Kate, Jane, Anna
'The Owl Who Was Afraid of the Dark' by Jill Tomlinson	Abbas, Kate, Bob, Tim, Tom, Pat, Anna, Beth
'The Worst Witch' by Jill Murphy	Emma, Mike, Chung, Seth, Pippa, Dave
'The Diary of a Killer Cat' by Anne Fine	Rob, Fred, Frank, Reuben

Strand: Reading Elements: Communicating LO 1; Understanding LO 3, 6

A Write 'yes' or 'no' for each sentence.

1. 'The Twits' was liked the most.
2. Kate does not like 'Fantastic Mr Fox'.
3. Abbas likes 'The Twits'.
4. Rob and Fred like 'The Diary of a Killer Cat'.
5. Chung and Beth like 'The Cat in the Hat'.

B Answer the questions.

1. How many books were in the survey?

2. Which book was liked the most?

3. Which book was liked the least?

4. How many children liked 'The Worst Witch'?

5. Does Dave like 'Fantastic Mr Fox'?

C Oral language

In pairs, take turns telling your news from the weekend. Use the planning grid below. Make sure you use time words. You might like to make a chart of useful words with your class.

When	Who	What	Where	Why	Feeling

On Saturday
First
Then
After that
Next
Finally

Strand: Reading Elements: Understanding LO 6; Exploring and Using LO 7, 8, 9
Strand: Oral Language Elements: Communicating LO 1, 2, 3; Exploring and Using LO 11, 13 14

33

Phonics /ie/ sound family – ie | /ue/ sound family – ue

A Read the real and silly words. Tick (✓) the real word in each box.

driep	pie	nie	priep
tried ✓	nie	lie	slien
smie	gried	rie	cried
clue	snue	queue	dissue
plue	frue	mue	hissue
skue	true	bue	tissue

B Tick (✓) the best sentence for each picture.

1. Sue cried when she spilled the glue. Sue cried when she could not get the glue.	
2. Dave had a plate of fries and fish. Dave had a bag of chips.	
3. Kate sat on the big, blue bed. Kate put a blue sheet on the bed.	
4. Reuben put fuel in the motorbike. Reuben stopped to get fuel for the jeep.	
5. Dad dried the blanket on the line. Dad dried the dishes left at the sink.	

Strand: Reading Element: Understanding LO 4, 5

Grammar – Past Tense Irregular Verbs

A Ring the correct spelling of each verb in the grid below. ✏️

push	share	hate	help	look

(pushed)	shareed	hateed	helped	lookeed
pusheed	shared	hated	helpeed	looked

Some verbs do not take 'ed' in the past tense. These are irregular verbs. We must learn these verbs off by heart.

Examples: run – Yesterday, the dog **ran** away.

 see – Last night, I **saw** a film.

B Write the correct word.

1. Yesterday, Jill _____ a fish pie. **make / made**

2. Last week, Reuben _____ me a pot of glue. **gave / give**

3. Last night, I _____ a packet of sweets. **ate / eat**

4. Dad _____ home very late last night. **come / came**

5. Last Tuesday, we _____ hot chocolate. **drink / drank**

C Dictation: Listen to your teacher and write the sentences. 👂

1. _____

2. _____

How did you do? 🙂 ⚪ 😐 ⚪ ☹️ ⚪

Writing Genre – Independent Writing

A Plan your weekend news.

Use the news planners to plan your weekend news. Include pictures and words to help you.

Friday News Planner

When	Who	What
Where	**Why**	**Feeling**

Saturday News Planner

When	Who	What
Where	**Why**	**Feeling**

B Write your news by yourself. Use more than one sentence. Make sure they are in the correct order.

Strand: Writing **Elements:** Communicating LO 1, 2; Exploring and Using LO 6, 7

A Letter to Santa

7

Phonics Game | /ai/ sound family – ai | /oa/ sound family – oa

A Before you begin the game, tick (✓) the sounds that you can read.

oa	ue	ie	ai	a_e	ee	oa
ai	ie	ee	oa	i_e	u_e	o_e

B Catch the elves!

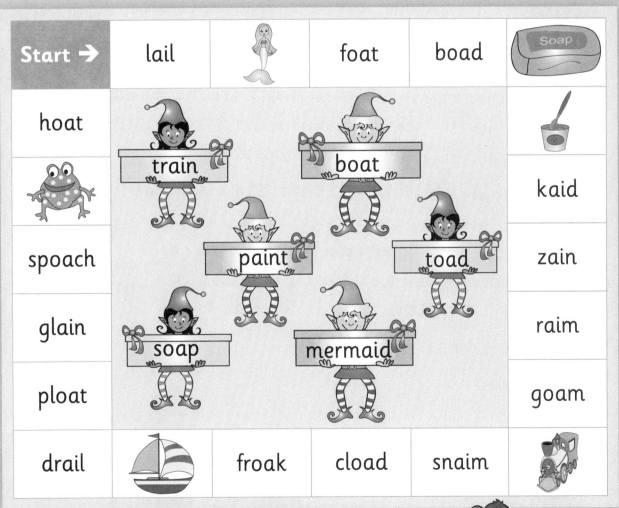

Start →	lail		foat	boad	Soap
hoat	train		boat		
					kaid
spoach	paint		toad		zain
glain	soap		mermaid		raim
ploat					goam
drail		froak	cload	snaim	

Try playing this at home again. All you need is a die and a set of counters.

Strand: Reading Element: Understanding LO 4, 5

Comprehension

STOP

Do you know what the **bold** words below mean? Can you explain them to your partner?

Look out for words that have **ai** or **oa** in the letter below.

A Letter to Santa

4 Oak Road,
Hilltree Town

Dear Santa,

I hope you are well. My little sister and I have been very good. I help my mum A LOT. Yesterday, my little sister, Bella, pulled our dog's tail. Then, our dog got into an **awful flap** and started chasing his tail around and around. **Suddenly**, the bucket of water Mum was using spilled all over the floor. Afterwards, I had to help Mum mop it all up.

Do you think I could have a train and a sailboat for Christmas and maybe a surprise? My little sister would like a **mermaid** doll. Mum would like a coat and Dad would like a new toaster. I am going to pop this letter in the **mail** to you.

Can't wait for Christmas Eve!

From Ben

P.S. I promise to put out a glass of milk and some scones with raisins for you. I know they are your favourite!

Strand: Reading Elements: Communicating LO 1; Understanding LO 4, 5, 6

A Match the words to make sentences.

Mum wants	a sailboat and a train.
Dad wants	a coat.
Ben wants	pull the dog's tail.
Bella likes to	a new toaster.

B Answer the questions.

1. Who wrote the letter?

_____

2. What kind of pet does Ben have?

_____

3. Who does Ben help at home?

_____

4. What does he want for Christmas?

_____

C Oral language

Make a word bank with your class about birthdays.
Think of words that remind you of your birthday.

_____	_____	_____
_____	_____	_____
_____	_____	_____

Strand: Reading Elements: Understanding LO 6; Exploring and Using LO 8, 9
Strand: Oral Language Element: Understanding LO 5

39

Phonics /ai/ sound family – ai | /oa/ sound family – oa

A Write the correct word.

1. When I fell, I groaned in _____ . **paid / pain**
2. Seth spilled the pot of blue _____ . **paid / paint**
3. I got a _____ as a present. **train / brain**
4. The _____ gave a croak in the pond. **coat / toad**
5. I put my raincoat on when it was _____ . **raining / rain**

B Follow the instructions or write the answer.

1. Put a dot on the snail.	
2. Cross out the biggest pot of paint.	
3. Cross out the biggest pot of blue paint.	
4. The train is _____ . The boat is _____ .	
5. The hen _____ six eggs.	
6. Ring the plate with toast and jam.	

Strand: Reading Element: Understanding LO 4, 5, 6

Grammar – Nouns

Nouns are naming words. They tell us the name of a person, a place, an animal or a thing. **Examples:**

 Name   **Place**   **Animal**   **Thing**

Finn   Dublin   reindeer   bells

Santa   North Pole   robin   present

A Write each noun in the correct box.

| Spain | present | robin | cracker | Luke |
| dog | Kildare | Orla | Alba | deer |

Name	**Place**	**Animal**	**Thing**

B Ring two nouns in each sentence.

1. Last week, Emily gave Hannah a present.

2. On Sunday, Hassan put gifts under the tree.

3. Yesterday, I went to the shops with Mum.

4. A few days ago, I pulled a cracker with Dad.

C Dictation: Listen to your teacher and write the sentences.

1. _____

2. _____

How did you do? 🙂 ⚪ 😐 ⚪ ☹️ ⚪

Strand: Writing Element: Understanding LO 3, 4, 5

Writing Genre – Independent Writing

A Write about your birthday.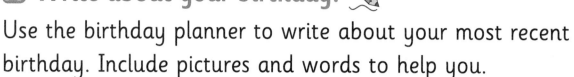

Use the birthday planner to write about your most recent birthday. Include pictures and words to help you.

Birthday Planner

When 🕐	Who 👪	What 📦
Where 🏡	**Why** ❓	**Feeling** 🙂🙁

B Write about your birthday by yourself. Use more than one sentence. Make sure they are in the correct order.

C Look over your writing again. Did you remember everything?

Strand: Writing **Elements:** Communicating LO 1, 2; Exploring and Using LO 6, 7

Revision and Assessment

Revision: Grammar and Phonics

Day 1

1. **Ring the word that needs a capital letter.**

   fintan came to school by bus.

2. **What letter comes next?**

   e, f, g, h,

3. **Is the underlined word a noun or a verb?**

   (a) I <u>put</u> the paint in the shed.

   Noun   Verb

   (b) The postman brings our <u>letters</u>.

   Noun   Verb

4. **Fill in the correct word.**

   make / made

   (a) Yesterday, I ____ muffins.

   (b) My mum likes to ____ cakes.

5. **Tick the real words.**

   green   blie

   traim   clue

Day 2

1. **Ring the words that need a capital letter.**

   the school is closed until january.

2. **What letter is missing?**

   l, m,   , o, p

3. **Is the underlined word a noun or a verb?**

   (a) We <u>went</u> shopping in town.

   Noun   Verb

   (b) I made a <u>card</u> for Grandad yesterday.

   Noun   Verb

4. **Fill in the correct word.**

   give / gave

   (a) Will you ____ the umbrella to Caleb?

   (b) I ____ my umbrella to Amy.

5. **Tick the real words.**

   flade   bleen

   choke   toaster

43

Revision: Grammar and Phonics

Day 3

1. **Ring the words that need a capital letter.**

   on monday, it will be my birthday.

2. **Ring the word that comes first in alphabetical order.**

   (a) scarf   hat   coat

   (b) nest   wing   egg

3. **Is the underlined word a noun or a verb?**

   (a) My dad is named <u>Samuel</u>.

   Noun   Verb

   (b) Our dog <u>chases</u> the cat.

   Noun   Verb

4. **Fill in the correct word.**

   eat / ate

   (a) Ben and Claire   all of the sweets.

   (b) I like to   popcorn when I go to the cinema.

5. **Tick the real words.**

   frue   chicken

   skate   blat

Day 4

1. **Ring the words that need a capital letter.**

   my friend visited spain last year.

2. **Ring the word that comes first in alphabetical order.**

   (a) kite   football   bike

   (b) pink   green   black

3. **Is the underlined word a noun or a verb?**

   (a) Did you see my <u>coat</u>?

   Noun   Verb

   (b) James went to the <u>park</u>.

   Noun   Verb

4. **Fill in the correct word.**

   come / came

   (a) Mum told me to   home at three o'clock.

   (b) I was late and   home at five.

5. **Tick the real words.**

   smoke   drong

   unwell   craid

Assessment: Phonics

A Follow the instructions or write the answer.

1. Cross out the plate of fish and chips.

2. Which ostrich is biggest?

3. Ring the cup of coffee and muffin.

4. Cross out the three black dots.

5. Which glass is broken?

6. Tick the shark with a shell.

7. What colour is the third crane?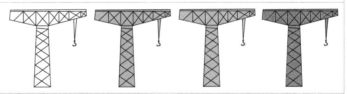

8. Match the man wearing a coat to the hat.

9. Which animal is last in the queue?

10. Put a dot on the tin of blue paint that has a paintbrush in it.

The Robin

What is it?

The robin is a small bird that lives in gardens.

What does it look like?

It is round and plump, with thin legs, short wings and a long tail. It also has a red chest.

wing

eye

tail

beak

leg

red chest

Where does it live?

The robin builds its nest in a tree using moss, twigs, grass and mud. You might also find a robin's nest inside a crack in a wall or an old tin can.

What does it eat?

It eats insects, spiders, earthworms and slugs.

Did you know?

A robin eating an earthworm

The mammy robin lays four to six eggs in the nest. The eggshells are very thin, so she must sit on the eggs to keep them safe and warm. After about two weeks, the baby robins hatch. The mammy robin hides the bits of broken eggshell so that cats will not know there are babies in the nest.

Assessment: Comprehension and Vocabulary

A **Answer the questions.**

1. Where does the robin live?

2. What does the robin like to eat?

3. What does the robin use to build its nest?

4. How many eggs does the mammy robin lay?

5. Who sits on the eggs to keep them safe?

6. Why does the mammy robin hide the broken bits of eggshell?

B **Vocabulary: Write the correct word.**

1. Megan gave a card   Sarah. **two / to / too**
2. We   happy we got no homework. **were / wear**
3. They put the box over   . **there / their**
4. Jack got his haircut   . **to / too / two**
5. You must   your hat. **were / wear**
6. What is   address? **their / there**

Assessment: Grammar

A Add capital letters and a full stop.

my favourite day of the week is friday

B Ring the word that comes first in alphabetical order.

1. unwell   sick   tummy
2. next   wing   egg
3. bike   kite   football

C Underline the verb in each sentence.

1. I ran all of the way home.
2. Anna cut up the cake.

D Ring two nouns in each sentence.

1. Shem has a pet dog.
2. I got a ball in the shop.

E Write the correct verb for each sentence.

1. I   a cup of coffee yesterday. **drank / drinked**
2. Last night, Dad   me a present. **gave / gived**
3. Tom   his leg on the chair. **bump / bumped**
4. In school, we   a robot. **made / maded**
5. Muhammad   all of the cake. **ate / eated**
6. I   to school last Tuesday. **walk / walked**

How did you do?

My Puppy

Phonics Game /ee/ sound family – **ea, y**

A Before you begin the game, tick (✓) the sounds that you can read.

ai		oa		y		ie		ee		a_e	
ea		ck		tw		u_e		dr		nt	

B Take me to the bone!

Start → clean summy granny treat

scream dream breezy brean

frosty lumpy lompy squeak vasty

stream drean nasty sticky squeal

grumpy twenty nearly tummy really Finish

Try playing this at home again. All you need is a die and a set of counters.

Poetry

Do you know what the **bold** words below mean? Can you explain them to your partner?

You can make the /ee/ sound with the letters **ee**, y or **ea**. Can you find any words in the poem with this sound?

My Puppy

It's funny
my puppy
knows just how I feel.

When I'm happy
he's **yappy**
and **squirms** like an **eel**.

When I'm grumpy
he's **slumpy**
and stays at my heel.

It's funny
my puppy
knows such a great deal.

By Aileen Fisher

A Tick (✓) the correct sentence.

1. The poet has a puppy.

   The poet has a kitten.

2. When the poet is happy, the puppy hides.

   When the poet is happy, the puppy jumps up and down.

3. When the poet is grumpy, the puppy licks its tail.

   When the poet is grumpy, the puppy stands by her side.

4. The puppy likes to bark when he is happy.

   The puppy likes to dig holes in the garden when he is happy.

B Answer the questions.

1. How might the poet look after the puppy?

   _____

2. Do you think a puppy is a good pet? Why?

   _____

3. What do you think the puppy does when the poet is sad?

   _____

C Oral language: Discuss the following with your class.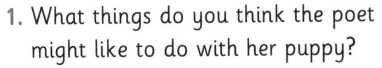

1. What things do you think the poet might like to do with her puppy?

2. (a) Do you know of any other poems about animals or pets?

   (b) Can you read them to the class?

Strand: Reading Elements: Understanding LO 5; Exploring and Using LO 8, 9
Strand: Oral Language Element: Exploring and Using LO 9, 10

51

Phonics /ee/ sound family – **ea, y**

Here are some new ways to spell the /ee/ sound:

sheep	happy	leaf

A Write the correct word.

1. Our teacher _____ us to read. **teaches / tweet**

2. My _____ was full after I ate the jelly. **eat / belly**

3. Holly had a cup of _____ and a cake. **tea / teeth**

4. The baby is asleep in the _____. **buggy / squeal**

B Follow the instructions or write the answer.

1. Put a dot under the messy bedroom.	
2. What colour are the jeans?	
3. The man likes to _____.	
4. Cross out the one that a baby does not use.	buggy nappy dolly happy
5. Ring the item you would not see at the seaside.	seagull seal bunny seashore

Strand: Reading Element: Understanding LO 4, 5

Grammar – Adjectives 1

Adjectives are describing words. They tell us more about a noun.

Examples: The **funny** man tells lots of jokes.

It was very **cold** yesterday.

Can you find the adjectives in the poem, 'My Puppy'?

A Ring the adjective in each sentence.

1. The green lorry drove down the road.

2. I had some yummy jelly and ice-cream for dessert.

3. Yesterday, the fat puppy fell asleep in the basket.

B Fill in the correct adjective.

bossy   happy   greedy   funny

1. My big brother tells me what to do. He is very   .

2. Sammy smiles a lot. He is very   .

3. My friend likes to tell jokes. He is very   .

4. Harry ate all of the sweets. He is very   .

Sammy

C Ring the adjectives. Underline the verbs.

1. The puppy got wet outside.   2. Holly had a hot cup of tea.

3. Molly ate a yummy peach.   4. Bobby had a bad dream.

D Dictation: Listen to your teacher and write the
     sentences.

1. _____

2. _____

How did you do? ☺ ○   ☹ ○   ☹ ○

Writing Genre – Poem

Pyramid Poem

A pyramid poem uses lots of adjectives and finishes with a short sentence.

Snake

A slithery snake
A slimy, slithery snake
A big, slimy, slithery snake
A hungry, big, slimy, slithery snake
Please don't eat me!

A **Pick an animal to write about.**

There are lots of adjectives for the animals below. If you want to write about a different animal, fill in the empty spaces.

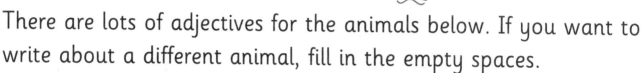

Cat	Dog	Fish	
soft	big	wet	
furry	little	slimy	
cute	funny	scaly	
cuddly	silly	pretty	
lazy	friendly	smooth	
scruffy	hairy	wriggly	

B **Write your own pyramid poem. Below is the recipe for the poem.**

Title animal
A adjective animal
A adjective, adjective animal
A adjective, adjective, adjective animal
A adjective, adjective, adjective, adjective animal
A short sentence to finish the poem.

Strand: Writing Elements: Communicating LO 1, 2; Exploring and Using LO 6, 7

The Little Red Hen

Phonics Game | /ou/ sound family – **ou** | /ur/ sound family – **ur**

A Before you begin the game, tick (✓) the sounds that you can read. 🖊

ea		ur		ai		ou		ue		y		a_e	
br		nd		ee		i_e		zz		wh		u_e	

B A spin and a roll

We all say nonsense words!

cloud	murr	burst	vaisin	ground	loast
purse	floud	count	vurst	drizzly	kive
nurse	murse	peach	swound	peanut	glave
peach	vount	chatty	nount	purr	bratty
proud	bround	found	vetty	toasty	joapy
church	lurse	hurt	naint	mouse	murt
raisin	glound	sound	dursty	boast	clound
round	vurst	burp	teanut	croaky	mussy

Try playing this with two players at home. Simply rub out the words you have ringed in class. This time, Player One can underline words and Player Two can ring them. Whoever fills a column first wins!

Strand: Reading Element: Understanding LO 4, 5

Comprehension

Do you know what the **bold** words below mean? Can you explain them to your partner?

Look out for words that have ou or ur in the story below.

STOP

The Little Red Hen

The Little Red Hen lived on a farm with her friends the dog, the cat and the duck.

One day, she was **pecking** the ground and she found some seeds.

"Who will help me plant these seeds?" she asked.

"We won't," said the dog, the cat and the duck.

"Then I will do it myself," said the Little Red Hen.

Her friends liked to lie in the sun all day. When it was time to cut the **wheat**, they would not help. When it was time to visit the **mill** to get the wheat **ground** into flour, they would not help. When it was time to bake the cake, they would not help. The poor Little Red Hen had to do it all by herself.

Finally, the Little Red Hen had a yummy cake.

"Who will help me eat the cake?" she asked.

"We will, we will, we will!" shouted the dog, the cat and the duck.

But the Little Red Hen said, "You lot are lazy sods! I think I will eat it all by myself!" And she did.

Strand: Reading Elements: Communicating LO 1; Understanding LO 4, 5, 6

A Fill in the correct word.

grew   share   duck   farm   cake   mill

1. The Little Red Hen lived on a _____ .
2. The dog, the cat and the _____ lay in the sun all day.
3. The seeds _____ into wheat.
4. The Little Red Hen went to the _____ .
5. The Little Red Hen baked a _____ .
6. The Little Red Hen did not _____ her cake.

B Answer the questions.

1. What did the Little Red Hen find on the ground?

_____

2. What did the Little Red Hen do with the seeds?

_____

3. Do you think the Little Red Hen is still friends with the dog, the cat and the duck? Why/Why not?

_____

4. How do you think the Little Red Hen felt when she ate all of the cake?

_____

C Oral language

Use the pictures on page 56 to help you retell the story of 'The Little Red Hen' in pairs. Don't forget to use time words.

Once upon a time
First
Next
Then
Finally

Strand: Reading **Elements:** Understanding LO 6; Exploring and Using LO 8, 9
Strand: Oral Language **Element:** Exploring and Using LO 11

57

Phonics /ou/ sound family – ou   /ur/ sound family – ur

A Look at each picture. Tick (✓) the correct word.

 surf / shout / sound	poppy / proud / purse	 nurse / neat / mouse
 furry / flour / found	 out / ouch / our	 scout / sour / shout

purrrrr

B Look at the picture. Write 'yes' or 'no' for each sentence.

1. The cat likes to purr.

2. The basket is round.

3. The kitten is curled up in the basket.

4. The basket is on the ground.

5. The mouse is running about the house.

6. The kitten has black fur.

7. It is a sunny day outside. It is not cloudy.

Strand: Reading **Element:** Understanding LO 4, 5

Grammar – Past Tense Verbs saw/seen, did/done

saw or seen?

I saw	I have seen
you saw	you have seen
he saw	he has seen
she saw	she has seen
we saw	we have seen
you saw	you have seen
they saw	they have seen

Always use **have** or **has** with **seen**.

did or done?

I did	I have done
you did	you have done
he did	he has done
she did	she has done
we did	we have done
you did	you have done
they did	they have done

Always use **have** or **has** with **done**.

A Tick (✓) the sentences that are correct.

1. I **saw** a little mouse.
2. Have you **seen** my coat?
3. We **seen** Dad surfing last summer.
4. Have you **saw** the film?
5. The dog has **seen** the cat.
6. They **seen** the nurse.

B Tick (✓) the sentences that are correct.

1. Have you **done** your homework?
2. They **did** not go home.
3. I **did** not like that man.
4. What have you **did**?
5. Molly **done** the dishes.
6. Billy has **done** his best.

C Dictation: Listen to your teacher and write the sentences.

1. _____

2. _____

How did you do? ☺ ○ ☹ ○ ☹ ○

Writing Genre – Parts of a Narrative

A Highlight the parts of a narrative.

Turn back to the narrative, 'The Little Red Hen' on page 56. Use yellow stickies or a highlighter pen to highlight the different parts of the narrative.

B Plan a story.

Fill in the story planner for 'The Little Red Hen'. Below are some words to help you.

cat   dog   duck   farm   one day   Little Red Hen
eat cake herself   found some seeds   friends would not help

Story Planner

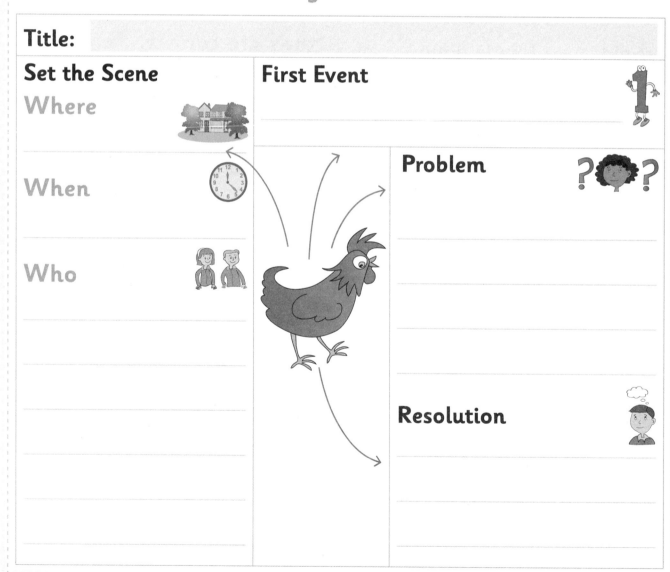

Title:

Set the Scene

Where

When

Who

First Event

Problem

Resolution

Strand: Writing **Elements:** Communicating LO 1; Exploring and Using LO 6, 7

Under the Bed

11

Phonics Game /ie/ sound family – **y** (fly), **igh**

A Before you begin the game, tick (✓) the sounds that you can read.

igh		ou		ur		ea		ai		ee	
y		oa		ue		a_e		ch		i_e	
nd		igh		ea		fr		y		sp	

B Snakes and Ladders

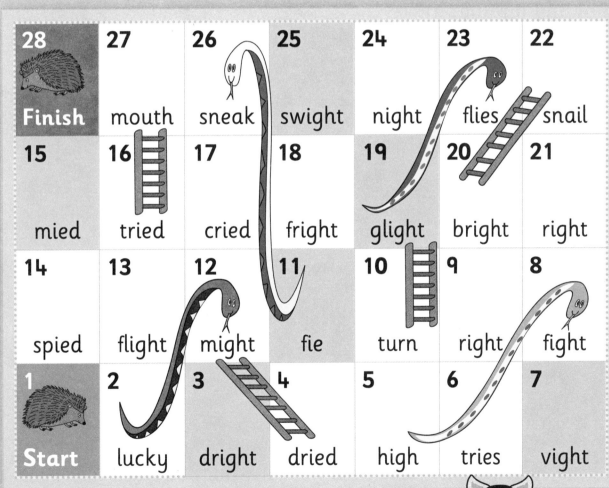

28 Finish	27 mouth	26 sneak	25 swight	24 night	23 flies	22 snail
15 mied	16 tried	17 cried	18 fright	19 glight	20 bright	21 right
14 spied	13 flight	12 might	11 fie	10 turn	9 right	8 fight
1 Start	2 lucky	3 dright	4 dried	5 high	6 tries	7 vight

Try playing this at home again. All you need is a die and a set of counters.

Comprehension

Do you know what the **bold** words below mean? Can you explain them to your partner?

STOP

You can make the /ie/ sound with the letters **ie**, **y** or **igh**. Can you find any words in the story with this sound?

Under the Bed

I get scared every night.

I'm fine if Dad is in my room, finishing my bedtime story.

I'm happy if Mum's there, saying, "Toby, are you sure you cleaned your teeth?"

I'm okay if Nana is sitting on the bed, singing our bedtime song: "Night, night, sleep **tight**. Hope the **fleas** don't bite."

And I'm alright if my brother Harry is **peeping** round the door.

But after they've gone, I get scared. I start to think there might be something under my bed. In the end, I get so worried that I call them up.

"Da-ad! Mu-um! Na-na! Har-ry!"

Harry came up. I felt like crying.

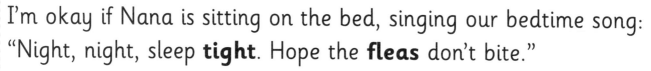

"Come on!" he told me. "Get out of bed and help me turn it over."

Harry began to **unscrew** the legs.

"Right," Harry said. "Now help me turn the bed back."

Now I sleep every night. If you don't have an under-the-bed at all, there can't be anything scary under it.

(From 'Under the Bed' by Anne Fine)

Strand: **Reading** Elements: Communicating LO 1; Understanding LO 4, 5, 6

A Number these sentences in the correct order.

	Toby and Harry take the legs off the bed.
1	Dad reads Toby a story.
	Harry comes upstairs.
	Toby thinks there is something under his bed.

B Answer the questions.

1. What does Nana do with Toby when he is going to bed?

_____

2. What is Toby afraid of?

_____

3. Who does Toby call when he is frightened?

_____

4. How did Harry help Toby?

_____

5. How would you help Toby?

_____

C Vocabulary: Write the correct word.

I thought there **were** three buns left.
were

where

wear

1. _____ do you want to go?
2. _____ is my coat?
3. I will _____ my hat and scarf.
4. The kittens _____ in the shed.

Phonics /ie/ sound family – y (fly), igh

Here are some new ways to spell the /ie/ sound:

p**ie**	n**i**n**e**	sp**y**	fr**igh**t

A Look at each picture. Tick (✓) the correct word.

	berry bite buy		feast fly fight		spy shy sky
	tight try tights		bright butterfly burst		fight five ferry
	might many my		night nurse nanny		might night nine

B Write the correct word.

1. I like to fly my _____ . **kite / bite**

2. At _____ , my dad turns out the lights. **bright / night**

3. It is not _____ to fight or tell lies. **right / high**

4. The little boy told us _____ he started to cry. **try / why**

5. My little sister is very _____ . **shy / cry**

Strand: Reading Element: Understanding LO 4, 5

Grammar – Alphabetical Order 2

A Rewrite each set of letters in alphabetical order.

1. F, A, S   2. Q, R, T
3. P, C, Z   4. D, L, X
5. T, W, C   6. J, D, A

B Number each set of words in alphabetical order.

1. hose	shed	garden	1
2. coach	bus	truck	
3. win	prize	first	
4. black	white	red	
5. banana	apple	plum	

C Rewrite each set of words in alphabetical order.

1. snail, spider, slug   ,   ,
2. sad, selfish, smile   ,   ,
3. pet, pig, panda   ,   ,
4. coffee, cheese, carrot   ,   ,
5. scarf, skirt, shirt   ,   ,
6. duck, deer, dog   ,   ,

D Dictation: Listen to your teacher and write the sentences.

1. _____

2. _____

How did you do? ☺ ◯   ☹ ◯   ☹ ◯

Writing Genre – Modelled and Shared Writing

A Create a comic strip. ✏️

In pairs, complete this comic strip with the story of 'The Three Billy Goats Gruff' or another fairytale.

Comic Strip

Where When Who	First Event
Problem	Resolution

B With your class, write the story of 'The Three Billy Goats Gruff' or another fairytale.

Strand: Writing **Elements:** Communicating LO 1, 2; Exploring and Using LO 6, 7

Snip Snip! 12

Phonics Game | /ue/ sound family – ew | /oi/ sound family – oi

A Before you begin the game, tick (✓) the sounds that you can read.

oi	ea	ur	ew	igh	y	ou
ai	oa	u_e	a_e	ew	oi	i_e

B Catch the frogs!

Start →	clew	voil		toin	rew
blewy	chew		toilet		
coilt		screw	blew		strewt
					broip
threwy		coin			
			soil		moise
pewy					
koilt		fewy		loint	mew

Try playing this at home again. All you need is a die and a set of counters.

Strand: Reading Element: Understanding LO 4, 5

Comprehension

Do you know what the **bold** words below mean?
Can you explain them to your partner?

Snip Snip!

Erin cut some paper. She pulled it open. She had a line of paper Erins, all holding hands. Erin loved her scissors. They were green with a frog on them. She loved **snipping** with them. Snip snip! Goodbye, **tassels** on the rug!

Snip snip! Goodbye, leaves on the plants! Erin looked at herself in the mirror.

Her hair was **raggedy**. Erin held up her long curls. Chop chop! Down they fell on the floor. She went into her little sister's room.

"Hi, Rosie," she said, waking up her little sister, "want a new **hairdo** like mine?"

Rosie giggled. Soon Rosie too had a fantastic new hairdo.

"Erin!" said Mum.
"What on earth are
you doing? Stop it
immediately!"

Mum was very cross.

"I'm making
things look
neat," said Erin.

"Neat?" said Mum. "You're making things look terrible."

"Now you and Rosie will have to wear hats," said Mum. "We are going to visit Grandma and Grandpa."

(From 'Snip Snip!' by Creina Mansfield)

Strand: Reading **Elements:** Communicating LO 1; Understanding LO 4, 5, 6

A Fill in the correct word.

leaves   frog   hair   cut

1. Erin's scissors had a _____ on them.

2. Erin _____ the tassels off the rug.

3. She snipped the _____ off the plant.

4. She chopped her little sister's _____ .

B Answer the questions.

1. What colour were Erin's scissors?

_____

2. What did Erin love to do with her scissors?

_____

3. What did Rosie do when Erin cut her hair?

_____

4. Who were they going to visit?

_____

5. How did Mum feel when she saw what Erin had done?

_____

C Vocabulary: Write the correct word.

1. Did you _____ the rain?

2. Put your books over _____ .

3. I can't _____ the song.

4. _____ is a book
   for Jan.

hear

↓

here

Strand: Reading **Elements:** Understanding LO 6; Exploring and Using LO 8, 9

Phonics /ue/ sound family – ew | /oi/ sound family – oi

Here are some new ways to spell the /ue/ sound:			Do you remember the /oi/ sound?
 statue	 ruler	 stew	 boil

A Read the real and silly words. Tick (✓) the real word in each box.

blewt	noit	jewt	soim
blew ✓	noise	jigh	smurry
blout	nigh	jewel	soil
screwt	point	coin	drewn
screw	poilt	coix	drew
scoit	pean	cly	dreen

B Fill in the correct word.

new   noisy   oil   rude   stew   soil   spoil   tortoise

1. Do not point your finger. It is _____.

2. Aseem planted some seeds in a pot of _____.

3. We made a big pot of _____ for dinner.

4. Mum put some _____ in the car.

5. Chen got a _____ bike as a present.

6. Those boys are very loud and _____.

7. Patrick keeps his pet _____ in a hutch.

8. Do not _____ the film by telling me what happened.

Strand: Reading Element: Understanding LO 4, 5, 6

Grammar – Adjectives 2

Remember:

Nouns are naming words. **Example:** chair	Verbs are action words. **Example:** run	Adjectives are describing words. **Example:** big

A Ring the best adjective for each picture.

yummy hot — small big — green wet — dry wet — hot fluffy — funny fast

soft sharp — loud broken — tired chatty — high spooky — warm cold — fat tall

B Ring the adjectives. Underline the nouns.

1. Andrew likes to ride his new bike.

2. We flew the red kite at the park.

3. The little spider ran across the bathtub.

4. The shy girl hid behind her mum's leg.

Hint! There are at least two nouns in each sentence.

C Dictation: Listen to your teacher and write the sentences.

1.

2.

How did you do? ☺ ◯ ☺ ◯ ☹ ◯

Strand: Writing Element: Understanding LO 3, 4, 5

Writing Genre – Independent Writing

A Plan a story.

Fill in the story planner for the story of 'Jack and the Beanstalk'.

| Jack | Once upon a time | giant | mother | cottage |

sold cow for magic beans   giant chased Jack   cut down

Story Planner

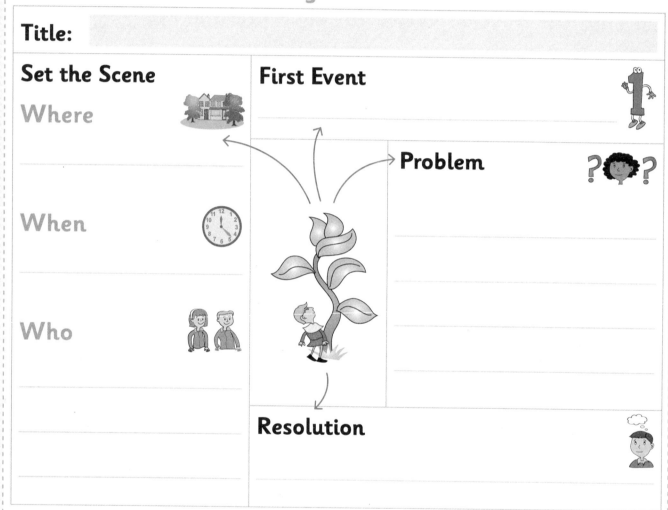

Title:

Set the Scene

Where

When

Who

First Event

Problem

Resolution

Ring some adjectives.	**Ring some verbs.**
big scary poor tall high	climbed ran grew hid cut

B Write the story of 'Jack and the Beanstalk' by yourself.

C Look at your story again. Did you remember everything?'

Strand: Writing Elements: Communicating LO 1, 2; Exploring and Using LO; 6, 7

Making a Flower Mobile 13

Phonics Game | /ou/ sound family – **ow** | /ai/ sound family – **ay**

A Before you begin the game, tick (✓) the sounds that you can read.

ay	ew	oi	ea	ow	ur	ou
oa	ay	ow	ie	ue	ck	ng

B A spin and a roll

We all say nonsense words!

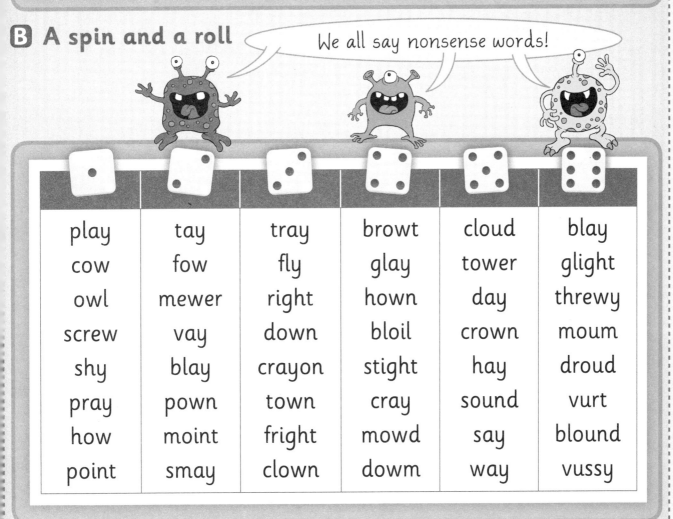

play	tay	tray	browt	cloud	blay
cow	fow	fly	glay	tower	glight
owl	mewer	right	hown	day	threwy
screw	vay	down	bloil	crown	moum
shy	blay	crayon	stight	hay	droud
pray	pown	town	cray	sound	vurt
how	moint	fright	mowd	say	blound
point	smay	clown	dowm	way	vussy

Try playing this with two players at home. Simply rub out the words you have ringed in class. This time, Player One can underline words and Player Two can ring them. Whoever fills a column first wins!

Strand: Reading Element: Understanding LO 4, 5

Comprehension

Do you know what the **bold** words below mean? Can you explain them to your partner?

STOP

Look out for words that have **ow** or **ay** in the procedure below.

How to Make a Flower Mobile

What you will need:

- clay
- a **rolling pin**
- a tray
- a lid from a big jar
- **flower-shaped cutters**
- a pen
- spray paint
- **twine**

Steps:

1. First, roll the clay out flat with a rolling pin.		
2. Next, push the jar lid into the clay to make the top part for the mobile.		
3. Then, push the flower cutters into the clay to make flowers for the mobile.		
4. Use the pen to poke a hole in the top of each flower.		
5. Then, poke some holes in the top part of the mobile.		
6. After that, lay everything on a tray to dry.		
7. The next day, spray paint the flowers.		
8. Finally, tie the flowers to the mobile using twine.		

Strand: Reading **Elements:** Communicating LO 1; Understanding LO 5, 6

A Number these steps in the correct order.

	Spray paint the flowers.	
	Press the jar lid and the flower cutters into the clay.	
1	Roll the clay out flat.	
	Use twine to tie the flowers to the mobile.	
	Let the clay dry.	

B Answer the questions.

1. What do you use to roll out the clay?

_____

2. How do you put a hole in each flower?

_____

3. Where do you put the flowers to dry?

_____

4. How do you paint the flowers?

_____

C Oral language

Play the game 'Simon Says' as a class.

1. In pairs, name the 'bossy' verbs after each instruction. Make a list of as many 'bossy' verbs as possible.

2. In pairs, give two instructions using time words, for example, 'First, put your hands on your head. Then, jump up and down'.

Strand: Reading Elements: Understanding LO 5, 6; Exploring and Using LO 7, 8, 9, 10
Strand: Oral Language Elements: Communicating LO 1, 3; Understanding LO 4, 5, 6

75

Phonics | /ou/ sound family – **ow** | /ai/ sound family – **ay**

Here are some new ways to spell the /ou/ sound:		Here are some new ways to spell the /ai/ sound:		

mouth	howl	nail	game	crayon

A Write the correct word.

1. Where did you _____ they went? **sow / say**

2. How much did you _____ for that? **now / pay**

3. I dried myself after my _____. **shower / towel**

4. The dog _____ at me. **gown / growled**

5. My sister likes to make a _____. **tower / trowel**

B Follow the instructions or write the answer.

1. Ring the vowels.	 e f g i a o w u y a	
2. What colour is the crayon?		
3. Join the two brown owls.		
4. Put a line under the smallest cow.		
5. Cross out the clown with a frown.		

Strand: Reading Element: Understanding LO 4, 5, 6

Grammar – 'Bossy' (Command) Verbs

When you played 'Simon Says', you used 'bossy' verbs. These are verbs that give orders.

Examples: **jump** **shout** **stand** **run**

A **Ring the 'bossy' verb in each sentence.**

1. First, get some paint and a paintbrush.

2. Next, paint the flower red.

3. Then, stick some petals onto the flower.

4. After that, draw some grass with a green crayon.

5. Finally, colour the soil brown.

> We use 'bossy' verbs when explaining how to make something.

B **Write the best 'bossy' verb to begin each sentence.**

> Boil the peas.

 Hop up and down.

1. _____ the banana. **Put / Peel / Paint**
2. _____ the carrots. **Drink / Chop / Glue**
3. _____ the pot with water. **Write / Fill**
4. _____ the kettle. **Boil / Eat / Bake**
5. _____ as fast as you can. **Use / Run**
6. _____ on one leg. **Stand / Clap / Pass**

C **Dictation: Listen to your teacher and write the sentences.**

1. _____

2. _____

How did you do? ☺ ○ 😐 ○ ☹ ○

Writing Genre – Parts of a Procedure

A Highlight the parts of a procedure.

Turn back to the procedure, 'How to Make a Flower Mobile' on page 74. Use yellow stickies or a highlighter pen to highlight the different parts of the procedure.

B Fill in the correct words.

diagrams   steps   title   what you need

How to Make a Flower Mobile

What you will need:	
▪ clay	▪ **flower-shaped cutters**
▪ a **rolling pin**	▪ a pen
▪ a tray	▪ spray paint
▪ a lid from a big jar	▪ **twine**

Steps:

1. First, roll the clay out flat with a rolling pin.

2. Next, push the jar lid into the clay to make the top part for the mobile.

3. Then, push the flower cutters into the clay to make flowers for the mobile.

4. Use the pen to poke a hole in the top of each flower.

5. Then, poke some holes in the top part of the mobile.

6. After that, lay everything on a tray to dry.

7. The next day, spray paint the flowers.

8. Finally, tie the flowers to the mobile using twine.

Strand: Writing **Elements:** Communicating LO 1; Exploring and Using LO 8

How to Plant Seeds

Phonics Game | /au/ sound family – **aw** | /ur/ sound family – **ir**

A Before you begin the game, tick (✓) the sounds that you can read.

aw		ir		ay		ow		y		ur	
ew		oi		ou		ue		a_e		i_e	

B Take me to the flowers!

Start → saw baw girl paw

mirl yawn chirp shirt

claw pay shirm first hirst

crawl glaw frown bird day

seesaw stir soil point howl Finish

Try playing this at home again. All you need is a die and a set of counters.

Strand: Reading Element: Understanding LO 5, 6

Comprehension

Do you know what the **bold** words below mean? Can you explain them to your partner?

STOP

Look out for words that have **aw** or **ir** in the procedure below.

How to Plant Seeds

What you will need:	Steps
• an old shirt • a **trowel** • a flowerpot or a bowl • soil • seeds • a spray bottle of water	1. First, put on an old shirt so you do not make a mess. 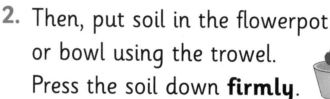 2. Then, put soil in the flowerpot or bowl using the trowel. Press the soil down **firmly**.  3. Next, **poke** a few holes in the soil with your finger.  4. Then, place seeds in the holes in the soil and **lightly** cover them with some more soil.  5. After that, **squirt** some water on the seeds.  6. Put the flowerpot on the **windowsill** and wait for the seeds to grow.  7. Finally, don't forget to wash your dirty hands. 

Strand: Reading **Elements:** Communicating LO 1; Understanding LO 4, 5, 6

A Number these steps in the correct order.

	Then, add the seeds.	
1	Put some soil in the flowerpot.	
	Give the soil some water.	
	Poke some holes in the soil.	
	Cover the seeds with some more soil.	

B Answer the questions.

1. What do you put in the flowerpot first?

_____

2. What do you put in the flowerpot after the soil?

_____

3. How do you poke holes in the soil?

_____

4. Where do you put the flowerpot while waiting for the seeds to grow?

_____

C Vocabulary: Write the correct word.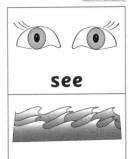

1. Did you _____ Jack?

2. I saw a ship out at _____.

3. The _____ was very choppy.

4. I will _____ my gran on Tuesday.

see

sea

Strand: Reading Elements: Understanding LO 6; Exploring and Using LO 7, 8, 9, 10

Phonics /au/ sound family – aw | /ur/ sound family – ir

A Look at the picture. Write 'yes' or 'no' for each sentence.

1. It is the girl's birthday.

2. The girl is giving a big yawn.

3. The baby likes to crawl.

4. There is a bird on the seesaw.

5. The bird likes to chirp.

B Look at the picture. Follow the instructions.

1. Draw a dot on the bird.

2. Draw some flowers on the lawn.

3. Draw some strawberries on the bush.

4. Draw a line under the first girl in the line.

5. Draw a ring around the third girl in the line.

Strand: **Reading** Element: Understanding LO 4, 5, 6

Grammar – a or an?

We use **a** when a word starts with a consonant.

Examples: a book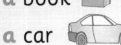

a car

We use **an** when a word starts with a vowel.

Examples: an elf

an umbrella

A Write 'a' or 'an' for each animal below.

1. owl 2. ant 3. tiger 4. elephant

5. panda 6. alligator 7. snake 8. ostrich

9. insect 10. whale 11. fish 12. octopus

B Read the lists. Write 'a' or 'an' for each word.

Equipment needed for an art activity:

1. paintbrush
2. pot of red paint
3. easel
4. pencil
5. eraser
6. tube of glue
7. ink pad

When we write lists, we must use 'a' or 'an'.

Ingredients needed for a fruit dessert:

1. apple
2. banana
3. handful of grapes
4. orange
5. apricot
6. handful of strawberries

C Dictation: Listen to your teacher and write the sentences.

1. _____

2. _____

How did you do?

Writing Genre – Modelled and Shared Writing

A In pairs, fill in the plan for how to make an Irish flag.

Title:

Tick what you will need.

paper		a lollipop stick		scissors	
glue		crêpe paper		a pencil	

Steps:

1.

Tick the words to use.

first   draw   make   put

2.

Tick the words to use.

then   next   pull   rip   tear

3.

Tick the words to use.

next   after that   stick   glue

4.

Tick the words to use.

after that   then   glue   stick

5.

Tick the words to use.

finally   wait   leave   dry

B With your class, write the procedure, 'How to Make an Irish Flag'.

Strand: Writing **Elements:** Communicating LO 1; Exploring and Using LO 6, 7

The Gosling Song

Phonics Game | /oi/ sound family – **oy** | /au/ sound family – **au**

A Before you begin the game, tick (✓) the sounds that you can read.

oi	ue	oy	au	o_e	ir	ay
oy	ew	igh	ur	au	ou	ee

B Catch the chicks!

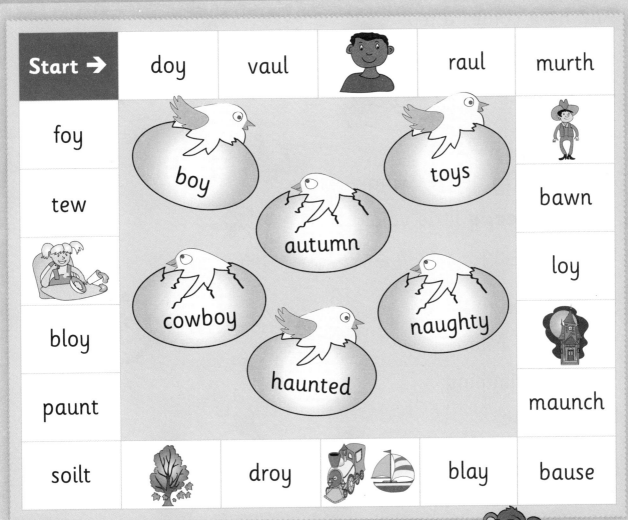

Start →	doy	vaul		raul	murth
foy		boy		toys	
tew					bawn
		autumn			loy
bloy		cowboy		naughty	
paunt		haunted			maunch
soilt		droy		blay	bause

Try playing this at home again. All you need is a die and a set of counters.

Strand: Reading Element: Understanding LO 4, 5

Poetry

Do you know what the **bold** words below mean?
Can you explain them to your partner?

The Gosling Song

What's that tapping?
Well, well, well,
A little baby **gosling**
Pecking at the shell.

Here comes a beak
And here comes a leg,
A little baby gosling
Hatching from its egg.

Out pops a head
And a **fluffy** yellow wing,
Then a **cheepy** little voice
Begins to sing.

Show me to the water,
Watch me, Mum,
See me swimming,
Here I come.

By Tony Mitton

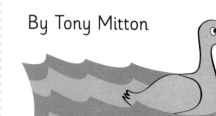

A Answer the questions.

1. How does the baby gosling break the eggshell?

_____

2. What colour is the baby gosling?

_____

3. Where does the baby gosling want to go?

_____

4. Who brings it to the water?

_____

B Oral language: Read the instructions below and make a chick with your class.

What you will need:		
• paper • yellow paint	• a plastic fork • googly eyes	• glue • an orange marker

Steps:			

1. First, put a blob of paint on the paper.	**2.** Then, use the fork to make a chick shape.	**3.** Next, add two eyes.	**4.** Finally, draw legs and a beak.

1. Retell how you made the chick. Don't forget 'bossy' verbs and time words.

2. Are there any other verbs or time words that you could use?

Strand: Reading Elements: Understanding LO 1; Exploring and Using LO 6
Strand: Oral Language Element: Exploring and Using LO 9, 11, 13, 14

Phonics | /oi/ sound family – oy | /au/ sound family – au

Here are some new ways to spell the /oi/ sound:

 soil

 boy

Here are some new ways to spell the /au/ sound:

 haunted

 yawn

A Look at each picture. Tick (✓) the correct word.

box
boy ✓
buy

toad
toilet
toy

hawk
haunted
handbag

autumn
awful
away

joy
job
jigsaw

loud
lawn
laundry

B Fill in the correct word.

naughty   laundry   paused   joy   cowboy   autumn

1. In _____, all of the leaves fall from the trees.

2. I was filled with _____ when I won the prize.

3. In our house, we all do chores. I do the _____.

4. My little brother likes to dress up as a _____.

5. That boy took all of the sweets. He is very _____.

6. We _____ the film last night when my gran called in to visit.

Strand: Reading Element: Understanding LO 4, 5, 6

Grammar – Plural – 'es'

If a word ends in **s**, **x**, **sh** or **ch**, we add **es** to make more than one.

Examples:

dress	fox	bush	bench 
dresses	foxes	bushes	benches

A Add 's' or 'es' to make each item below plural.

1. one peach   six

2. one grape   seven

3. one sandwich   three

4. one spoon   two

5. one glass   two

6. one plate   three

7. one box   two

8. one dish   four

B Add 's' or 'es' to make each item below plural.

To make a rubbish monster, you will need:

1. 2 big   (box)   2. 1 packet of   (crayon)

3. 2 bin   (bag)   4. 1 packet of   (marker)

C Dictation: Listen to your teacher and write the sentences.

1. _____

2. _____

How did you do? ☺ ◯   ☺ ◯   ☹ ◯

Strand: Writing Element: Understanding LO 3, 4, 5

Writing Genre – Independent Writing

A Fill in the plan for how to make a spring chick.

Title:

Tick what you will need.

yellow paint	a paintbrush	glue
a plastic fork	a marker	paper
googly eyes	scissors	

Ring the time words you could use.

first   then   next   after   finally

Ring the 'bossy' verbs you could use.

put   use   make   draw   add   stick

Write the time words and 'bossy' verbs for each step.

1. _____

2. _____

3. _____

4. _____

B Write the procedure, 'How to Make a Spring Chick', by yourself.

C Look over your procedure again. Did you remember everything?

Strand: Writing Elements: Communicating LO 1; Exploring and Using LO 6, 7

Butterfly Hill Farm 16

Vocabulary – Revision of Homophones

A to / two / too

1. I have a pet cat _____ .

2. I have _____ new puppies at home.

3. "Would you like _____ come?" asked Zara.

B there / their

1. Will you put that over _____ ?

2. "I must put all of the bags over _____," moaned Thomas.

3. They rode _____ bikes to the park.

C were / where / wear

1. We don't know _____ the dog hid his bone.

2. I will _____ my new outfit to the party.

3. We _____ very sad when school finished for the holidays.

D hear / here

1. Did you _____ Conrad sing?

2. "_____ is an invitation to my party," said Jack.

3. I think I can _____ a noise inside the shed.

E see / sea

1. "Did you _____ the news last night?" asked Gavin.

2. I didn't _____ Ella yesterday, as she was sick.

3. We went on a trip to the _____ with our class.

Comprehension

STOP

Do you know what the **bold** words below mean? Can you explain them to your partner?

You can make the /au/ sound with the letters **al**. Look out for words with **al** or **er** in the poster below.

Butterfly Hill Farm

Bigger and better **tropical** house filled with **exotic** plants, butterflies and interesting moths!

Butterflies flying **freely** all around you!

Sheltered picnic spot
Children's playground

Free talk on butterfly **habitats** at:
1:00 p.m.   3:00 p.m.

Small framed butterflies for sale in the gift shop

See our petting corner with:

- snakes

- big snails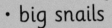

- stick insects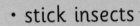

- tarantula spiders

TICKET PRICES:
Adult €8
Child €5
Family €25
O.A.P. €6
Under 5s free

Open for the summer holidays
Email: butterflyfarm@flutterfly.com
Give us a call on 01 8401432
Address: Butterfly Hill Farm,
Tree Top Hill, Co. Kerry

Why not take a walk in our **walled** garden?

Strand: Reading **Elements:** Communicating LO 1; Understanding LO 4, 5, 6

A Answer the questions.

1. Where is Butterfly Hill Farm?

_____

2. How much is an adult ticket?

_____

3. Where can you eat your lunch?

_____

4. What would you see in the tropical house?

_____

5. How can you contact Butterfly Hill Farm?

_____

6. What animal would you like to pet in the petting corner?

_____

B Oral language

Walking debate: Would you like to go on a school tour to Butterfly Hill Farm?

1. As a class, put two lines on the floor and label one 'yes' and the other 'no'.

2. Stand on the line that matches your answer.

3. Now, take turns explaining why you would or wouldn't like to visit Butterfly Hill Farm.

I would not really like to visit Butterfly Hill Farm, as I'm terrified of spiders.

Strand: Reading Element: Exploring and Using LO 6, 8, 9
Strand: Oral Language Elements: Communicating LO 1, 2, 3; Exploring and Using LO 8, 9, 13

93

Phonics | /au/ sound family – al | /ur/ sound family – er

A Tick the correct word for each sentence.

1. Sam likes to walk on the _____ .

   walk   walking   wall

2. Casper got the butter and pepper for _____ .

   drummer   digger   dinner   dagger

3. My little sister sometimes mixes up her numbers and _____ .

   litters   ladder   lantern   letters

4. I gave my little sister a _____ ball.

   stalk   small   stall

5. In class, we must not _____ while we do our work.

   talk   tall   talking

6. Last summer, Lauren saw a small _____ .

   gather   grasshopper   gutter   golfer

7. Dad lost his screwdriver and his _____ .

   hopper   helper   hamster   hammer

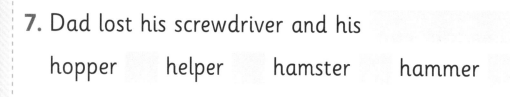

8. When I grow up, I want to be a singer or a _____ .

   dagger   digger   drummer   duster

Grammar – Future Tense Verbs 1

The future tense is what will happen. We must add the word **will** to a verb.

Examples:

I **will** swim	we **will** swim
you **will** swim	you **will** swim
he/she **will** swim	they **will** swim

A Write each verb in the future tense.

1. look   I will look

2. sit

3. smile

4. make

5. play

6. paint

7. go

8. jump

B Write each sentence in the future tense by changing the verb in brackets.

1. I (have) a picnic lunch.

_____

2. I (pet) the snake in the petting corner!

_____

3. The bus driver (drive) us there.

_____

C Dictation: Listen to your teacher and write the sentences.

1. _____

2. _____

How did you do? ☺ ◯ ☹ ◯ ☹ ◯

Strand: Writing **Element:** Understanding LO 3, 4, 5

Writing Genre – Parts of an Invitation

A **Read and discuss the invitation below with your class.**

> We invited Mark's dad, Mr Smith, as a helper on our school tour.

Dear Mr Smith,

We would like to invite you to join our school tour. We will be visiting Butterfly Hill Farm on Friday the 10th of May. We will be leaving school at 9 o'clock in the morning. You will need to bring a packed lunch and a raincoat.

Will you be able to help out?

From,

First Class

B **Fill in the correct words.**

who it is to   who it is from   time   where   when

Dear Mr Smith,

We would like to invite you to join our school tour. We will be visiting Butterfly Hill Farm on Friday the 10th of May. We will be leaving school at 9 o'clock in the morning. You will need to bring a packed lunch and a raincoat.

Will you be able to help out?

From,

First Class

Strand: Writing Elements: Communicating LO 1; Exploring and Using LO 8

Holiday Checklist 17

Vocabulary – Revision of Homophones

A Read each sentence and ring the correct word. ✏️

1. Will you put all of the boxes over **here** / **hear** please?

2. It was raining and we **were** / **where** / **wear** soaking wet.

3. "Can I go **to** / **two** / **too** the park after school with Aisling?" asked Sasha.

4. My friend Emma likes to collect shells by the **see** / **sea**.

5. "Don't forget to **were** / **where** / **wear** your hat," called Dad.

6. Oscar got **to** / **two** / **too** new footballs for his birthday.

7. I saw **there** / **their** mum at the shops yesterday.

8. "Did you **here** / **hear** the thunder last night?" asked Claire.

9. "Can I have some cake **to** / **two** / **too**?" asked Zaya.

10. I did not **see** / **sea** you at the playground yesterday.

11. Isaac ate all of the sweets and **there** / **their** were none left.

12. I think I know **were** / **where** / **wear** you left your purse.

Comprehension

Do you know what the **bold** words below mean? Can you explain them to your partner?

STOP

Look out for words with **or** in the checklist below.

Holiday Checklist

THINGS TO PACK:

Clothes

shorts ☐
T-shirt ☐
swimming togs ☐
flip-flops ☐
sun hat ☐
torch ☐

Toiletries

shampoo ☐
soap ☐

Stuff for the beach

beach bag ☐
sunglasses ☐
beach towel ☐
snorkel ☐
flippers ☐
book ☐
reading glasses ☐
sun cream ☐

IMPORTANT THINGS – DO NOT FORGET!

passport ☐
credit cards ☐
car keys ☐
airport parking ticket ☐

JOBS TO DO BEFORE I GO:

1. Mow the grass ☐
2. Borrow **snorkel** and **flippers** from Lorna ☐
3. Check in **online** ☐
4. Lock all of the windows ☐
5. Empty the bins in the kitchen ☐
6. Leave a set of keys with Nora ☐

THINGS TO PUT IN MY CASE IN THE MORNING:

toothbrush ☐
toothpaste ☐
phone charger ☐

Strand: Reading **Elements:** Communicating LO 1; Understanding LO 4, 5, 6

A Answer the questions. ✏️

1. What clothes will they pack?

_____

_____

2. How many jobs must they do before they go?

_____

3. What three items will they put in their case in the morning?

_____

4. What do you think the snorkel and flippers are for?

_____

5. Why do you think they are bringing a phone charger?

_____

6. Do you think an adult or child wrote this list? Give reasons for your answer.

_____

_____

_____

B Oral language: The Invite Game 💬

1. As a class, stand in a circle.

2. One pupil walks around the circle, stops behind another pupil and has a conversation, inviting them to sports day or on a school tour. Make sure to include details such as where you are going and when it will take place.

3. Finish the conversation and shake hands. Then, each pupil runs in opposite directions. The first pupil to sit on the empty spot wins!

4. The remaining pupil continues the game.

Phonics /or/ sound family – or

The letters **o** and **r** make the /**or**/ sound.

horse	thorn	fork	tortoise

Don't forget to use capital letters and full stops.

A Unscramble each sentence and rewrite it.

1. forgot I bag popcorn my of

_____

2. Cork Jordan born in was

_____

3. forty My is dad old years

_____

4. Rory I a have present for

_____

5. put on I my and T-shirt shorts

_____

6. storm Orla's kite away blew in the

_____

7. has Dora hamster tortoise a and a

_____

8. pick up We Morgan will airport from the

_____

Strand: Reading Element: Understanding LO 3, 4, 5

Grammar – Future Tense Verbs 2

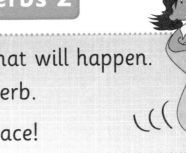

Remember: The future tense is what will happen. We must add the word **will** to a verb.

Example: I **will** win the sack race!

A Change the verbs in brackets to the future tense.

1. We   (have) our school sports day tomorrow.

2. I   (take part) in the egg-and-spoon race.

3. Next, we   (sit) and eat our lunch.

4. Finally, we   (pull) the rope in the tug of war.

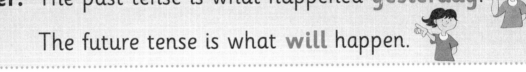

Remember: The past tense is what happened **yesterday**.
The future tense is what **will** happen.

B Read each sentence and tick the correct tense.

1. Yesterday, I went on my school tour.   **Past**   **Future**

2. We will get our holidays soon.   **Past**   **Future**

3. Next week, Abel will go to visit his friend. **Past**   **Future**

4. At the weekend, I played tennis with Vish. **Past**   **Future**

5. Last Friday, I painted the shed.   **Past**   **Future**

C Dictation: Listen to your teacher and write the sentences.

1. _____

2. _____

How did you do? 🙂 ◯ 😐 ◯ 🙁 ◯

Writing Genre – Independent Writing

A Plan an invitation to an adult at home, inviting them to your school sports day.

To / Dear			
What	**Where**	**When**	**Time**

Anything else?

From

Some useful words:

| football pitch | Saturday morning | 9 o'clock | May |
| P.E. hall | half past 9 | June | 1st / 2nd / 3rd / 4th |

Some useful verbs:

we will start   we will finish

we will have   you will need to bring

B Write an invitation to an adult at home, inviting them to your school sports day.

C Look over your invitation again. Did you remember everything?

Strand: **Writing Elements:** Communicating LO 1, 2; Exploring and Using LO 6, 7

Revision: Grammar and Phonics

Day 1

1. **Tick each sentence if it makes sense.**
   (a) My cat likes.
   (b) I went to the park.

2. **Number each set in alphabetical order.**
   (a) cake   bake   tin
   (b) Mum   Dad
       Gran

3. **Ring the adjective and underline the nouns.**
   (a) Dad got a new car.
   (b) My best friend sits beside me.

4. **Write 'a' or 'an'.**
   (a) Take   umbrella with you.
   (b) Do you have   book?

5. **Write 's' or 'es'.**
   (a) I have two red (pen).
   (b) Put the three (box) there.

6. **Tick the real words.**
   seesaw   tortoise
   smigh   snerry

Day 2

1. **Tick each sentence if it makes sense.**
   (a) I can run home.
   (b) Do you like.

2. **Number each set in alphabetical order.**
   (a) dog   deer   duck
   (b) cat   cub   crab

3. **Ring the adjective and underline the nouns.**
   (a) That big book belongs to Rory.
   (b) I put on my red T-shirt.

4. **Write 'a' or 'an'.**
   (a) Can you pass me   apple, please?
   (b) I ate   banana as a snack.

5. **Write 's' or 'es'.**
   (a) I got two (bunch) of grapes.
   (b) We have five little (kitten).

6. **Tick the real words.**
   oyber   screw
   deach   twirl

Revision: Grammar and Phonics

Day 3

1. **Ring the words that need a capital letter.**
   (a) i saw patrick on sunday.
   (b) last may, i broke my arm.

2. **Number each set in alphabetical order.**
   (a) beach   boat
   ball
   (b) picnic   park
   play

3. **Ring the best adjective.**
   (a) The elephant has a short / long trunk.
   (b) A zebra has blue / black stripes.

4. **Ring the correct word.**
   (a) She wishs / wishes she had a new bike.
   (b) I made three cakes / cakees.
   (c) I carried two boxs / boxes upstairs.
   (d) I dropped all of the glasss / glasses.

5. **Tick the real words.**
   curly   fratter
   surprise   dound

Day 4

1. **Ring the words that need a capital letter.**
   (a) i would like to visit my friend in kerry.
   (b) will you come to play on saturday?

2. **Number each set in alphabetical order.**
   (a) sea   swim   sun
   (b) head   hat   hot

3. **Ring the best adjective.**
   (a) I felt very tired / silly after the run.
   (b) It was very high / hot today.

4. **Ring the correct word.**
   (a) We planted five trees / treees.
   (b) My pet dog watchs / watches the cat.
   (c) The dog hid two bones / bonees.
   (d) I got two bunchs / bunches of grapes.

5. **Tick the real words.**
   florch   rainbow
   crayon   sluetill

Assessment: Phonics

A Follow the instructions or write the answer.

1. Ring the red, hairy monster.

2. Tick the thickest brown crayon.

3. Match the puppy to the bone.

4. Underline the round, yellow cake.

5. Which tower is tallest?

6. Draw a box around the flower under a rainbow.

7. Cross out the small, empty bucket.

8. Draw a bow on the largest clown.

9. Ring the numbers and underline the capital letters.

      2   D   e
    a   6   7
J   M

10. The crayon is
and the biggest pen is
.

Flat Stanley

Breakfast was ready.

"I will go and wake the boys," Mrs Lambchop said to her husband, George Lambchop.

Just then their younger son, Arthur, called from the bedroom he shared with his brother Stanley.

"Hey! Come and look! Hey!" Arthur said.

He pointed to Stanley's bed. Across it lay the enormous bulletin board that Mr Lambchop had given the boys a Christmas ago, so they could pin up pictures and messages and maps. It had fallen during the night, on top of Stanley. But Stanley was not hurt. In fact he would still have been sleeping if he had not been woken by his brother's shout.

"What's going on here?" he called out cheerfully from beneath the enormous board.

Mr and Mrs Lambchop hurried to lift it from the bed.

"Heavens!" said Mrs Lambchop.

"Gosh!" said Arthur.

"Stanley's flat!"

"As a pancake," said Mr Lambchop.

(From 'Flat Stanley' by Jeff Brown)

Assessment: Comprehension and Vocabulary

A Answer the questions.

1. What are the names of the two brothers?

2. What had fallen on Stanley during the night?

3. Who gave it to them?

4. Who woke Stanley up?

5. How did Stanley feel when he woke up?

6. How did his parents feel when they saw him?

7. If you were Stanley's parent, what would you have done next?

B Vocabulary: write the correct word.

1. _____ did you find the ball? **were / where / wear**

2. _____ is a present for Mariam. **hear / here**

3. I was _____ tired to go out and play. **to / too / two**

4. We went on a trip to the _____ side. **see / sea**

5. They went to visit _____ grandad. **their / there**

6. _____ a sun hat in the sun! **were / where / wear**

Assessment: Grammar

A Rewrite with capital letters and a full stop.

we will go to spain on our summer holidays

B Ring the word that comes first in alphabetical order.

1. beep   jeep   horn

2. tiger   ape   snake

3. duck   quack   chick

C Is the underlined word a noun, an adjective or a verb?

	Noun	Adjective	Verb
1. The <u>dog</u> jumped up and down.			
2. It was so <u>hot</u> we stopped for ice-cream.			
3. Dad <u>made</u> sandwiches for the picnic.			

D Write 'a' or 'an'.

1. I ate ____ apple for my lunch yesterday.

2. Dad brought ____ umbrella in case it rained.

3. Mum put ____ box on the shelf.

4. "Do you have ____ envelope?" asked Shane.

5. ____ dog ran out on the road in front of us.

E Write the plural (more than one) of each word.

1. one book   two

2. one glass   two

3. one ostrich two

4. one bush   two

How did you do?

Dictation

Red indicates phonics covered in the unit. Green indicates grammar.

Purple indicates an additional activity or a question revising grammar taught recently.

Differentiation

For weaker pupils, it is possible to shorten any of the dictation sentences to as little as two to three words, e.g. We had a big chat in class. ➔ We had a chat in class. ➔ a big chat ➔ a chat

Unit 1

1. We had a big chat in class.
2. I got a train and a doll.

What do we use at the start/end of a sentence?

Unit 2

1. We went to Dublin.
2. Fred likes to jump in the pond.

What needs a capital letter in sentence 1?

What needs a capital letter in sentence 2?

Unit 3

1. On Sunday, I like to bake a cake.
2. I went for a ride on Dad's bike.

What needs a capital letter in sentence 1?

What needs a capital letter in sentence 2?

Unit 4

1. Do not come home late.
2. It was very hot in June.

What needs a capital letter in sentence 2?

Unit 5

1. I had to sweep up the broken glass.
2. Dave drove the jeep up the street.

What should a sentence end with?

Are these sentences talking about today or yesterday? What tense is this?

Unit 6

1. I cried when I did not get a pie.
2. Sue had a tube of blue glue.

How many capital letters are there in sentence 1? What word always gets a capital letter?

Are these sentences talking about today or yesterday? What tense is this?

Can you ring the verb in the sentence 2?

How many verbs are there in sentence 1?

Unit 7

1. Joan painted the snail blue.
2. I moaned when my train fell.

Ring the verbs.

What do we add to some verbs to allow them to talk about the past?

Unit 9

1. That greedy boy took all of the sweets.
2. It was very windy and stormy today.

Ring the verbs and underline the adjectives.

Can you think of other suitable adjectives to use to describe the weather?

Unit 10

1. Did you hear that loud sound?
2. The furry mouse hurt his tail.
What must go at the end of sentence 1? Why?
Ring the verb and underline the adjective in sentence 2.
Can you think of another verb/adjective you could use?

Unit 11

1. The sky was very cloudy last night.
2. My mum got such a fright and jumped.
Underline the adjective in sentence 1. Can you think of another suitable adjective?
Ring the two verbs in sentence 2. Are they talking about today/present or yesterday/past?

Unit 12

1. Can I go to the toilet, please?
2. My dad got a packet of new screws.
What must go at the end of sentence 1? Why?
Ring the verb and underline the adjective in sentence 2.
Can you think of another suitable verb/adjective that you could use?

Unit 13

1. Dry yourself with a towel after your shower.
2. The brown owl made a nest in the hay.
Can you find the 'bossy' verb in sentence 1?
Can you find the adjective in sentence 2? Can you think of another suitable adjective?

Unit 14

1. First, draw a bird and an owl.
2. Then, draw an ant and a cow.
Can you find the 'bossy' verb in sentence 1?
Can you list the time words? Can you think of other suitable time words to use?
Why do we write 'an owl' and 'an ant'?

Unit 15

1. That boy Paul took all of the paintbrushes.
2. How many toys does that boy have?
Can you find the verb in sentence 1? Can you think of another suitable verb?
Why does 'paintbrushes' get 'es' to make it plural?
Why does 'toys' just get 's' to make it plural?

Unit 16

1. We will have two football matches.
2. It will be much hotter in the summer.
Are these sentences about today, yesterday or tomorrow? How do you know?
Why does 'matches' get 'es' to make it plural?

Unit 17

1. We will not forget our passports.
2. Jordan will get the hammer and torch for Dad.
Are these sentences about today, yesterday or tomorrow? How do you know?
If this happened yesterday, how could you change the sentence to show that?